EX LIBRIS

VINTAGE CLASSICS

THE PRINCE

Niccolò Machiavelli was born in Florence on 3 May 1469. He served the Florentine Republic as the Secretary of the Second Chancery, but was expelled from public life when the Medici family returned to power in 1512. His most famous work, *The Prince*, was written in an attempt to gain favour with the Medicis and return to politics. Machiavelli died on 21 June 1527.

NICCOLÒ MACHIAVELLI

The Prince

TRANSLATED AND ANNOTATED BY
Peter Constantine

VINTAGE BOOKS
London

Published by Vintage 2009

16

Copyright © 2007 by Random House, Inc.

The Prince was first published in 1532

This translation was first published in Great Britain by
Vintage in 2008

Vintage
Random House, 20 Vauxhall Bridge Road,
London SW1V 2SA

www.vintage-classics.info

Addresses for companies within The Random House Group Limited
can be found at: www.randomhouse.co.uk/offices.htm

The Random House Group Limited Reg. No. 954009

A CIP catalogue record for this book
is available from the British Library

ISBN 9780099518495

Penguin Random House is committed to a sustainable future for
our business, our readers and our planet. This book is made from
Forest Stewardship Council® certified paper.

Printed and bound in Great Britain by Clays Ltd, Elcograf S.p.A.

CONTENTS

Niccolò Machiavelli to His Magnificence Lorenzo de' Medici[1]

Those who wish to win the favour of a prince will generally approach him with gifts of what they value most or what they believe will most delight him. Hence we see princes being offered horses, arms, vestments of gold, precious stones, and similar accoutrements worthy of their grandeur. Wishing to present myself to Your Magnificence with a token of my deepest respect, I have found among my possessions nothing that I value or esteem higher than my knowledge of the deeds of great men. I have acquired this knowledge through my long experience of modern affairs and a lifelong study of ancient times, all of which I have weighed and examined with great diligence and brought together into this small volume, which I am now offering to Your Magnificence. Though I deem this work unworthy of being in Your illustrious presence, my confidence in Your benevolence persuades me that it will be accepted, and that Your Magnificence will recognize that I cannot offer You a greater gift than the prospect of Your understanding in the shortest period all that I have experienced and learned over so many years and with so much danger and hardship. I have not filled this volume with pompous rhetoric, with bombast and magnificent words, or with the unnecessary artifice with which so many writers gild their work. I wanted nothing extraneous to ornament my writing,

1. Lorenzo de' Medici (1492–1519) was the grandson of Lorenzo the Magnificent.

for it has been my purpose that only the range of material and the gravity of the subject should make it pleasing. Nor do I wish it to be thought presumptuous that a man of low and humble condition like myself should presume to map out and direct the government of princes. But just as a cartographer will descend into the plains in order to study the nature of the mountains, and will then climb the highest peaks in order to study the low-lying land, so, too, only an exalted prince can grasp the nature of the people, and only a lesser man can perceive the nature of a prince.

I hope therefore that Your Magnificence will accept this humble gift in the spirit in which it is offered. Should You condescend to read and consider it carefully, You will perceive in its pages my profound desire that Your Magnificence will rise to the greatness that Fortune and Your qualities promise. And should Your Magnificence deign to look down from the lofty summit of Your eminence to these lowly depths, You will see how I have suffered undeservedly Fortune's great and continuing malignity.

CHAPTER ONE

OF THE KINDS OF
PRINCIPALITIES THAT EXIST,
AND HOW THEY CAN BE ACQUIRED

All states, all dominions that rule or have ruled over men, are or have been either republics or principalities. Principalities are either hereditary, with a long-established bloodline, or new. And the new principalities are either entirely new, as Milan was to Francesco Sforza,[2] or are like limbs added to the hereditary state of the prince who acquires them, as the Kingdom of Naples was to the King of Spain.[3] States obtained in this way are accustomed either to living under a prince, or to being free. They are acquired either with the arms of others, or with one's own, either by chance or by skill.

2. Francesco Sforza (1401–66) was a soldier of fortune who became Duke of Milan in 1450.
3. Ferdinand the Catholic (1452–1516), King of Aragon, also became Ferdinand III of Naples in 1504.

CHAPTER TWO

OF HEREDITARY PRINCIPALITIES

I will not discuss republics, as I have already done so at some length elsewhere. I shall only concentrate on principalities, and shall weave together the threads I have already laid out. I will show how these principalities can be governed and maintained.

First, states that are hereditary and tied to the bloodline of their prince are easier to maintain than new ones. It is enough not to diverge from the practices of one's forebears, and to handle unforeseen issues as they arise. If such a prince is of at least average ability he can retain his position of power, so long as no extraordinary or excessive force deprive him of it. If this prince is deprived of his state, he will find he can reacquire it if any misfortune befalls the usurper.

In Italy we have the example of the Duke of Ferrara, who resisted the assaults of the Venetians in 1484 and of Pope Julius II in 1510, for the simple reason that he had inherited an ancient principality.[4] A hereditary prince has less cause to mistreat his subjects, and so is more loved by them. If unusual vices do not make him hated, it is to be expected that he will be loved by his people.

The long continuum of the dominion obliterates the memories and issues that make men yearn for innovation, for one change will inevitably forge a link to another.

4. In fact, Duke Ercole d'Este of Ferrara managed to end the war with Venetians in 1484, while his son Duke Alfonso managed to stay in power despite excommunication and an ongoing war with the papal forces.

CHAPTER THREE

OF MIXED PRINCIPALITIES

It is in the new principality that the difficulties lie. First, if the principality is not completely new, but is like a limb or extension added to another principality (in which case we could almost call the whole state a mixed principality), its volatility stems mainly from a difficulty inherent in all new principalities. This is that men will willingly change their ruler in the hope that they will fare better, a hope that leads them to take up arms against their old ruler. But in this they are deceived, because, as they invariably discover, their lot under a new ruler is inevitably worse. This is the result of another natural and basic inevitability: that you cannot avoid offending those whose new ruler you are, both with your armed soldiers and with innumerable other provocations that come in the wake of a conquest. You end up making enemies of all those you have offended during your conquest of the principality, and you find that you cannot keep the friendship of those who helped you to power, since you cannot satisfy them in the way they had envisioned. Furthermore, you cannot take strong measures against them, as you are indebted to them. Even with the most powerful army, if you want to invade a state, you need the support of the people. It was for these reasons that King Louis XII of France was quick to occupy Milan, and just as quick to lose it. Duke Ludovico's own forces were enough to win Milan back the first time, because the same masses that had opened the gates for Louis, finding themselves misled in their hopes for a better future, could not endure the new prince's offences.[5]

It is a fact that once a prince acquires a rebellious state for the second time, it also proves harder to lose that state a second time.[6] This is because the prince who seizes the opportunity of the rebellion has fewer scruples about securing his position by punishing offenders, flushing out suspects, and strengthening all the places where he is weakest. In this sense, it was enough for a Duke Ludovico to make a little noise along the borders for Louis XII to lose Milan the first time. But for him to lose Milan a second time the whole world had to unite against him, defeat his army, and chase it out of Italy.[7] This followed from the causes I have already laid out. Nonetheless, both the first and second time, Milan was taken from him.

The general reasons for the first loss have been discussed. It now remains to discuss the second, and to see what recourse someone in Louis's position could have taken to maintain himself more securely in his new acquisition. I must stress that the states a prince acquires and adds to his own are either of the same country and language, or are not. If they are it is much easier to retain them, particularly if they are not used to freedom. To hold them securely, it is enough to extinguish the line of the previous prince who ruled them. As for the rest, if the new acquisition's former state of affairs is kept and there is no difference in customs, men will live quite peacefully, as we have seen in Burgundy, Brittany, Gascony, and Normandy, which for a long time now have all belonged to France. Although there is some difference in language, their customs are similar, and their people get along with one another quite easily. He who acquires such states and wishes to retain them has to make sure of two things: that the bloodline of their former princes is extinguished, and that their laws and taxes remain the same. This way, the prince's new state merges with the old, quickly becoming a single body.

But difficulties arise when you acquire states in a land with differ-

5. Louis XII occupied Milan in September 1499, but was ousted in February 1500 by Ludovico Sforza. Louis, however, managed to recapture Milan within two months.
6. Once Louis XII recaptured Milan, it remained under his rule until 1512.
7. The Holy League of 1511, organized by Pope Julius II, was an anti-French coalition that included Spain, Venice, the Holy Roman Empire, England, and the Swiss. The League managed to drive the French out of Milan in May 1512.

ing languages, customs, and laws. To keep these states, you need good fortune and much diligence. One of the best and quickest solutions is for the new prince to go and live in his new state. This makes the possession more durable and secure. The Turk did this in Greece.[8] With all the other measures he took to keep Greece in his possession, had he not gone to live there he would not have succeeded, because once the prince is established within his new state he is able to see problems as they arise and can remedy them. If he is not there, problems become obvious only once they are dire and can no longer be remedied. Furthermore, if he is present, his new state will not be looted by his officials, and his new subjects can enjoy immediate access to their prince. This will give them more reason to love him if they are on his side, and to fear him if they are not, and foreign powers wishing to attack his state will respect him more. Hence, if the prince lives in his new state, it is difficult for him to lose it.

Another efficient remedy is to set up colonies in one or two places that will act as the shackles of your new state. If you do not set up colonies, you will have to send a great number of troops to secure it, while a colony can be established and maintained at negligible cost. The only subjects who will be affronted are those whose fields and houses will be confiscated to be given to the new colonists. But these dispossessed subjects make up only a small part of the state and will end up poor and dispersed, and so can do no harm. The rest of your new subjects will not be affronted (and hence will be acquiescent), but will also be frightened of transgressing, worried that they too might be dispossessed. I conclude that colonies do not cost much, are loyal, and will cause less trouble. And as I have already mentioned, those you dispossess cannot harm you, as they will be poor and dispersed. In short, men must either be flattered or eliminated, because a man will readily avenge a slight grievance, but not one that is truly severe. Hence, the offence done a man must be of the kind that cannot incur vengeance.

If you choose armed forces instead of colonies, you will spend more and will have to squander all the income from the new state in order to pay the army. This will turn the acquisition into a loss, and all your

8. The Turks occupied Constantinople in 1453, and in 1457 transferred the capital of the Ottoman Empire from Edirne to Constantinople.

new subjects will end up offended, since an army, constantly on the move and constantly requartered, hurts the whole state. Everyone feels the pain, and everyone becomes your enemy. And these are enemies who can harm you, because though they have been defeated, they remain on their own ground. So in every sense, using armed forces is as useless as setting up colonies is useful.

It is also important when a prince has conquered a foreign state that he become the protector of the surrounding weaker powers, and do all he can to weaken the stronger ones. He must take precautions so that no foreigner equal in power manages to enter his new state. If he should enter, it will be because he was brought in by discontented factions driven by ambition or fear. We saw this in the case of the Aetolians who introduced the Romans into Greece;[9] and in every other province in which the Romans set foot, it was with the help of some of the inhabitants. The order of things is that the moment a powerful invader takes over a state, all the weaker factions within it join forces with him, spurred on by their envy of the ruler who had wielded power over them before. In other words, the new prince has no trouble winning the weaker factions over, because they will willingly become part of his new state. He has only to see to it that they do not gain too much power and authority. With his forces and their favour, he can easily bring down those who are powerful so that he will remain the only arbiter in the land. He who does not follow this course will quickly lose all he has gained, and will be plagued by infinite difficulties while he holds power.

The Romans were careful to follow these principles in the provinces they conquered, establishing colonies, supporting the less powerful without increasing their strength, undercutting the strong, and not letting powerful foreigners gain standing there. Greece serves as a perfect example. The Romans supported the Achaeans and the Aetolians, weakened the Kingdom of Macedonia, and chased out Antiochus.[10] Yet despite the help that the Achaeans and the Aetolians

9. The Aetolian League, a federation of cities north of the Gulf of Corinth, had become one of the leading military powers in Greece by the fourth century BCE. In 211 and 200–197 BCE the Aetolians joined Rome in its war against Philip V of Macedon.

10. The Achaean League, a federation of cities in the Peloponnesus, entered an alliance with Rome in 198 BCE against Philip V of Macedon, at the time the most powerful ruler in Greece. The alliance temporarily gave the Achaeans and the Aetolians (see previous footnote) domi-

provided, the Romans did not permit them to expand their territories. Nor did Philip's subtle persuasions induce the Romans to become his friends without undercutting him. And all of Antiochus's power still did not persuade the Romans to consent to his ruling over any state within their territories. The Romans did what every wise prince must do: They kept their eyes trained not only on present problems but also future ones, which must be anticipated with great care, because when one sees these problems approaching they can still be remedied, whereas if one waits for them to arrive it will be too late to administer medicine. The illness will have become incurable. As physicians say of consumption: In the first stages it is easy to cure though hard to detect, but with the progress of time, if not detected or treated, consumption becomes easy to detect but hard to cure. This can also be said of the affairs of state. If one recognizes evolving ills in advance (for which one must be far-sighted), one can cure them quickly. But if they are left to develop until they are plain for all to see, it will be too late for remedies.

The Romans recognized potential difficulties in advance and always remedied them in time. They never let problems develop just so they could escape a war, for they knew that such wars cannot be avoided, only postponed to the advantage of others. Consequently, the Romans chose to wage war on Philip and Antiochus in Greece so that they would not have to do so in Italy, even though they could have avoided war with either of them for a while. But they chose not to. The Romans never liked the dictum we constantly hear from the wise men of our day, that time will take care of things. The Romans preferred to take care of things by means of their own skill and prudence, because time will sweep everything before it and can bring good things as well as bad, bad things as well as good.

But let us return to France, and see if her king did any of the things we have discussed. I shall speak of Louis XII, not of Charles, as Louis held his acquisitions in Italy for a longer period, which gives us the opportunity to evaluate his progress with greater clarity. We will see how he did the exact opposite of what one must do to maintain a foreign state one has acquired.

---

nance in Greece. But within a few decades they were degraded to weak protectorates of Rome. Antiochus the Great (242–187) created a vast empire in Asia Minor and the East, but was finally defeated by Rome in the Battle of Magnesia in 190 BCE.

Louis XII managed to enter Italy through the ambition of the Venetians, who wanted to acquire half the state of Lombardy by his coming. I do not wish to censure the king's course of action: He wanted to gain a footing in Italy, and did not have any friends there. In fact, as all doors were shut to him on account of King Charles's actions,[11] Louis XII had to make friends wherever he could, and he would have succeeded in this course had he not made a number of mistakes elsewhere. Once he had acquired Lombardy, King Louis quickly regained the reputation that Charles had cost him. Genoa yielded, and the Florentines rushed to become his friends, as did the Marquis of Mantua, the Duke of Ferrara, Bentivoglo, the Countess of Forlì, the Lords of Faenza, Pesaro, Rimini, Camerino, Piombino, and the men of Lucca, Pisa, and Siena. The Venetians quickly realized the rashness of the course they had chosen: In order to gain two holdings in Lombardy, they had helped King Louis gain dominion over two-thirds of Italy.

Let us consider how easily Louis could have maintained his reputation in Italy if he had observed the aforementioned rules. He could have remained secure had he stood by his friends, who, because they were many, weak, and afraid (some of the Church, some of the Venetians), would have been forced to remain at his side. With their help he could have kept in check those who remained powerful. But no sooner did he set foot in Milan than he did the exact opposite, helping Pope Alexander to occupy the province of the Romagna. What Louis did not realize was that with this move he weakened himself, alienating his allies and those who would readily have rushed into his arms, and strengthened the Church, adding to its spiritual power, which gives it such authority, a prodigious amount of temporal power.

Having made this initial mistake, Louis was forced to continue making mistakes, so that in the end, in order to curb Pope Alexander's ambitions and stop him from becoming the ruler of Tuscany, he was forced to invade Italy. It was not enough that Louis strengthened the Church and pushed away his friends, but because he coveted the Kingdom of Naples, he decided to share it with the King of Spain. The result was that, whereas he had been the only authority in Italy, he now

11. Charles VIII of France had marched through Italy in 1494 to occupy Naples, which he had inherited from the Angevins. He was crowned King of Naples in 1495, but was ousted in the Battle of Fornovo that same year by Ludovico Sforza, Emperor Maximilian I, the pope, and King Ferdinand II of Aragon, who formed the League of Venice.

introduced a powerful companion to whom ambitious and dissatisfied men could turn. Instead of leaving a king in Naples who would be a puppet, he drove him out and brought in a king who was powerful enough to drive Louis out.[12]

The wish to acquire is a most natural thing, and men who manage to acquire are always applauded (or at least not blamed) when they succeed. What is an error and worthy of blame is when a man cannot acquire something, but desires to obtain it in any way he can. If Louis, for instance, could have conquered Naples with his own forces, he should have done so. If he could not, he should have desisted, and not opted for sharing Naples with another power. It is excusable that he shared Lombardy with the Venetians, because that was how he managed to secure a foothold in Italy, but that he shared Naples merits blame, because it cannot be excused by any such necessity.

In other words, Louis XII made the following five mistakes: He destroyed the smaller powers; he helped a single power in Italy to gain strength;[13] he brought a powerful foreigner into Italy;[14] he did not go to live there; and he did not establish colonies. These errors would not have redounded on him in his lifetime had he not committed a sixth error by depriving the Venetians of their state. Had he not strengthened the Church or brought Spain into Italy, undercutting the Venetians would have been necessary in order to weaken them. But having made the first moves, Louis should never have consented to Venice's ruin. A strong Venice would have kept the others out of Lombardy, either because Venice would not have allowed anyone but itself to become Lombardy's ruler, or because the others would not have wanted to take Lombardy from France simply in order to hand it over to Venice. Furthermore, they would not have had the spirit to fight both France and Venice. Were someone to argue that King Louis ceded the Romagna to Pope Alexander and the Kingdom of Naples to Spain in order to avoid war, I would respond with the point I have already made: You must never allow disorder to develop in an attempt to avoid war, as this way you are not escaping war, but simply postponing it

12. In 1500, Louis XII signed the Treaty of Granada with Ferdinand II for a partition of the Kingdom of Naples. But tensions soon grew between Louis and Ferdinand over the partition, and by 1504 Louis had been ousted from Naples.

13. Pope Alexander.

14. King Ferdinand.

to your own disadvantage. And if others were to allege that Louis had pledged his support in the pope's campaign in gratitude for the Church's annulment of his marriage and the hat of Rouen,[15] I will counter that with some later points concerning the pledges of princes and how they should be regarded.

In short, Louis lost Lombardy because he did not observe some of the principles followed by others who have taken territories and managed to keep them. Nor is any of this a miracle, but quite ordinary and reasonable. I spoke to the Cardinal of Rouen about this matter at Nantes, when Valentino (that was how Cesare Borgia, the son of Pope Alexander, was known to his friends) was occupying the Romagna. When the cardinal declared that the Italians did not understand warfare, I replied that the French did not understand the state; because had they understood the state, they would not have let the Church rise to such power. And experience has shown that the strength of the Church and of Spain in Italy was brought about by France, and that France's ruin was brought about by them. From this one can draw a general rule that is almost always true: He who helps another man to power is setting himself up for ruin, because that power has been brought about by either diligence or force, both of which are suspect to the man who has newly become powerful.

15. Louis XII had been granted an annulment of his marriage to Jeanne de Valois, and a cardinalate for his minister, Georges d'Amboise, Archbishop of Rouen.

CHAPTER FOUR

WHY DARIUS'S[16] KINGDOM, WHICH ALEXANDER HAD OCCUPIED, DID NOT REBEL AGAINST ALEXANDER'S SUCCESSORS AFTER HIS DEATH

Considering the difficulties of retaining a newly acquired state, one marvels at how in a few years Alexander the Great managed to become the ruler of Asia and, having occupied it, died.[17] It would seem reasonable that after his death the territories he had acquired would have rebelled. And yet Alexander's successors did retain these territories, and had no difficulties other than those that arose among themselves, difficulties sparked by their own ambition. My point is that all the principalities in history have been governed in two ways: either by a prince and his servants, in which case the ministers who help him govern do so by his favour and concession, or by a prince and a group of barons, who hold their rank not by his favour but by the rights of their bloodline. These barons have their own states and subjects, who recognize them as their lords and have a natural affection for them.

In those states where a prince and his servants govern, the prince has more authority, as in all his territory there is no man who is considered superior to him. And if subjects obey a minister, they obey him as an official of the prince, and not out of particular affection.

Examples of these two kinds of government in our times are the

16. Darius III (d. 330 BCE) was the last king of Persia's Achaemenid dynasty. His empire was conquered by Alexander the Great in a series of battles from 334 to 331 BCE.
17. Alexander the Great (356–23 BCE), King of Macedonia, had within a decade conquered the Persian Empire and parts of northern India by the time he died at the age of thirty-four.

Turk and the King of France. The Turk's monarchy is governed by a single ruler, and everyone else is his servant. Dividing his kingdom into *sanjaks,* or provinces, he sends out governors, changing them at his pleasure. But the King of France is at the centre of an ancient multitude of lords, recognized by their subjects and loved by them. These lords have their own dominions, which the king can take from them only at his peril.

If one considers these two states, one finds it difficult to acquire that of the Turk, but easy to keep once it is won. It is difficult to conquer because there are no barons who can be called on to help the conqueror, nor is there hope for a rebellion of the Turk's entourage. This springs from the reasons I have mentioned previously. As all the Turk's men are dependents and bondsmen it is harder to corrupt them; and if they are corrupted, they prove of little use, as they do not have the populace behind them for the reasons I have mentioned. Consequently, whoever attacks the Turk should expect to find a united front, and must rely more on his own power than on the disorder of others. But once the Turk has been utterly defeated on the battlefield so that he cannot regroup, there is nothing left to fear but his own bloodline. Once that is extinguished, nobody remains to be feared, as there is no one who has credit with the people. Just as the victor could not expect anything from the Turk's men before the victory, he has nothing to fear from them afterwards.

The opposite happens in kingdoms like France, which you can conquer with ease by winning over some baron of the realm, because there are always those who are dissatisfied and desire change. They can open the way for you and help you to victory. But afterwards, when you try to maintain yourself in your new acquisition, you will face infinite difficulties both from those who helped you and from those you oppressed. Nor is it enough for you to extinguish the bloodline of the former prince, because there remain those lords who aspire to be leaders of a new regime. And as you will be unable either to please them or destroy them, you will lose the state whenever the opportunity to seize it from you arises.

If we look at Darius's kingdom, we find that its government was similar to that of the Turk. Therefore, Alexander needed first to strike at it in full force and achieve a decisive victory, after which, with Darius dead, the state, for the reasons I have already mentioned, stayed firmly in Alexander's grip. And Alexander's successors, had they been united, could have enjoyed this state in complete idleness. No turmoil broke out in their territories except for the turmoil they themselves provoked. But states organized like France cannot be possessed with such ease. This was also the reason for the frequent rebellions against the Romans in Spain, France, and Greece, because of the many old principalities in those territories. While the memory of those principalities lasted, the Romans were always tenuous in their possession. But ultimately, with the power and continuum of the empire, the memory died out and they became secure possessions. Later, when the Roman governors began fighting among themselves, each could take back part of the provinces according to how much power he had acquired in these territories. And since the bloodline of their old princes had been extinguished, the Roman governors were the only rulers these states recognized.

Considering all these issues, one should not be surprised at the ease with which Alexander kept his acquisitions in Asia, and the difficulty others had in conserving theirs (like Pyrrhus,[18] to name one of many). This is not a matter of the victor's skill, but of the different characteristics of the state he conquers.

---

18. King Pyrrhus of Epirus (319–272 BCE) fought energetically to expand his empire, seizing territories from Macedonia and Rome. His costly military accomplishments, however, resulted in his inability to hold on to his new acquisitions, giving rise to the modern phrase 'Pyrrhic victory': a victory at too great a cost.

CHAPTER FIVE

How one should govern cities or principalities which lived under their own laws before being conquered

When an acquired state has been accustomed to living in freedom under its own laws, there are three ways of securing it. The first is to destroy it; the second, to move there oneself; the third, to let it live with its own laws, exacting a tribute and creating within it a regime of a selected few who will keep it friendly toward you. As the regime of the state has been created by the new prince, it knows it cannot exist without his goodwill and power, and must do everything to maintain him. The best way to keep a city accustomed to living freely is through its citizens.

Consider, for example, the Spartans and the Romans. The Spartans occupied Athens and Thebes, creating a state governed by a few (though they lost this state again). The Romans, on the other hand, destroyed Capua, Carthage, and Numantia, and therefore did not lose them. They also wanted to occupy Greece in almost the same way the Spartans had occupied Athens and Thebes, making it free and with its own laws. This did not work, and the Romans ended up having to destroy many of Greece's cities in order to keep the province. In fact, the only secure way of keeping such a city is to destroy it. And whoever becomes the ruler of a city that is used to living free without destroying it can expect to be destroyed by the city. Because when such a city rebels, it always waves the banners of liberty and its former government, which are not forgotten with the passage of time or through any benefits bestowed by the new ruler. Notwithstanding what a new prince does or anticipates, if the inhabitants are not dispersed or driven into quarrelling factions, they will never forget the former government or order of things, and will quickly revert to it at every opportunity (as did Pisa after a hundred years of servitude to the Florentines). It is a different matter when cities or states are accustomed to living under a prince and his bloodline is extinguished, as on one hand they are used to obeying, and on the other they do not have their former prince. They will not be capable of uniting to elect a prince from among themselves, and they do not know how to live in freedom without a prince. Consequently, they are slower at taking up arms, and a new prince can win and secure them with greater ease. But in republics there is more vitality, more hatred, and more desire for revenge. The memory of former freedom simply will not leave the people in peace. In this case the safest course is for the prince either to destroy them or to go and live there himself.

CHAPTER SIX

OF NEW PRINCIPALITIES ACQUIRED
THROUGH ARMS AND SKILL

No one will be surprised if I cite a few eminent examples in speaking of principalities that are completely new in both prince and government. Men will always follow paths beaten by others, and proceed in their actions by imitation. But as they are rarely able to keep to these paths, or to match the skill of those they imitate, a prudent man should always set out on paths beaten by those who are truly great and worthy of imitation. This way, even if his own skill does not attain the same heights, he can at least expect to achieve some of the effect. A wise archer, for instance, will perceive that the distance of the target he intends to hit is too far off, and, knowing the extent of his bow's capacity, will aim quite a bit higher, not so that he will reach that height with his arrow, but so that he will gain his objective by aiming above it. The point I wish to make is that maintaining a principality that is entirely new, where there is a new prince, depends entirely on the skill of that prince. And because turning from a private citizen to a prince presupposes skill or good fortune, it would seem that either of these two factors will alleviate many of the difficulties. And yet he who has relied less on good fortune to acquire his principality has a better prospect of keeping it. Things also become much easier when the new prince does not have another state, and is obliged to live in his new acquisition.

But to come to those who have become princes through their own skill and not through chance, I would say that foremost among them are Moses, Cyrus, Romulus, and Theseus.[19] One ought perhaps not to count Moses, as he was a mere executor of the will of God; he must nevertheless be admired, if only for the grace that made him worthy of speaking to God. But let us consider Cyrus, and the others who acquired or founded kingdoms. They are all most admirable. If one weighs their actions and the measures they took, it is clear that they are not very different from those of Moses, who had such a great preceptor watching over him. If we examine their actions and lives, we see that the only gift that Fortune accorded them was the opportunity that gave them the substance they could mould into any form they pleased. Without that opportunity, their skill would not have flourished, and without that skill, the opportunity would have presented itself in vain. In other words, it was essential for Moses to find the people of Israel pining under the Egyptian yoke, so that they could emerge from slavery and be willing to follow him. It was vital for Romulus not to remain in Alba but to be exposed at birth,[20] so that he would become King of Rome and founder of the nation. It was crucial for Cyrus to find the Persians unhappy under the Empire of the Medes, and for the Medes to have grown soft and effeminate from a long period of peace. Theseus could not have demonstrated his skill had he not found the Athenians dispersed. Consequently, those opportunities favoured these men, and with their skill they seized the opportunity, with the result that their nations were ennobled and prospered.

Those who become princes through such skill acquire their principality with difficulty, but retain it with ease. The difficulties they have in acquiring the principality arise in part from the new order they are forced to introduce to set up their state and ensure their own security. Nothing is harder to do, more dubious to succeed at, or more dangerous to manage, than making oneself a ruler and introducing a new order. This is because he who introduces the new order makes enemies of all those who have done well under the old, and finds only half-hearted defenders in the men who would do well under the new. This half-heartedness arises in part from these men's fear of adversaries who

19. Machiavelli often uses these historical figures as examples of princely skill and ability. (See *The Prince*, chapters 16 and 26.)

20. Romulus, one of the legendary founders of Rome, had been ordered to be exposed to death as an infant by his uncle, King Amulius of Alba. According to legend, Romulus and his brother, Remus, were then raised by a wolf.

have the law on their side, and in part from the incredulity of man. Men intrinsically do not trust new things that they have not experienced themselves. Consequently, when enemies of the new order find any chance to attack the prince, they will attack him in full force, while men who benefit from the new order will defend him half-heartedly. Hence the prince is in a precarious position.

It is therefore necessary when examining this matter to ascertain whether the prince introducing the new order can act alone or must depend on others. In other words, he must seek help or use force to achieve his innovations. If he seeks help, he will always end up badly and accomplish nothing. But if he relies on his own skill and can use force, the innovator will rarely be in harm's way. This is why all armed prophets were successful, while unarmed prophets came to ruin. Another factor that must be considered is that a populace is always erratic. It is easy enough to win the people over, but difficult to keep their allegiance. Therefore, matters must be arranged in such a way that when the populace no longer believes, a prince can compel them to believe by force. Moses, Cyrus, Theseus, and Romulus would not have been able to make their people observe their laws for long without the force of arms, as we have seen in our own times with Girolamo Savonarola,[21] who came to ruin with his new order when the multitude lost belief in him. Savonarola did not have a system for holding on to those who had believed in him, nor did he have a system for making those believe who did not. Therefore, rulers like Savonarola have great difficulty in proceeding; their path is strewn with difficulties that they must overcome through prowess. Once they overcome these difficulties, the populace begins to venerate them. And once these rulers have eliminated those who resent their achievement, they remain powerful, secure, honoured, and content.

To these illustrious examples I would like to add a less eminent one, but one that is to some extent comparable, which might suffice for all other similar cases. It is the example of Hiero of Syracuse, who from private citizen became Prince of Syracuse.[22] In his case, Fortune did not accord him more than an opportunity. The people of Syracuse

21. Girolamo Savonarola (1452–98) was a charismatic Christian preacher who, after the fall of the Medici in Florence in 1494, ruled Florence as the leader of a strict and sober republican government until he was executed in 1498.
22. Hiero II of Syracuse (d. 216 BCE).

were oppressed, and so elected him their general, after which he proved himself worthy of being made their prince. He had so much skill, even as a private citizen, that someone who wrote about him says: *Quod nihil illi deerat ad regnandum praeter regnum* (He lacked nothing to make him a ruler except a kingdom).[23] Hiero eliminated the old army and set up a new one, abandoned old friendships for new ones, and on the foundation of these new soldiers and friends realized that he could build any edifice. It took much effort for him to acquire his state, but little to keep it.

23. Machiavelli quotes an altered line from Justin's *Epitome of the Philippic History of Pompeius Trogus* (Book XXIII, chapter 4): *Prorsus ut nihil ei regium deesse praeter regnum uideretur.*

CHAPTER SEVEN

OF NEW PRINCIPALITIES
ACQUIRED BY THE ARMS AND BY
THE GOOD FORTUNE OF OTHERS

Private citizens who become princes by good fortune alone do so with little effort, but maintaining their position requires a great deal of effort. They have no difficulty in getting there, because their way is easy; the difficulties arise once they arrive. These are rulers who acquire a principality through money or by favour of a grantor. This was the case with many rulers in the cities of Ionia and the Hellespont in Greece, where Darius, in order to ensure his security and glory, created princes who would hold these lands.[24] There were also private citizens who became rulers by bribing soldiers. Such men depend on the will and good fortune of whoever has granted them their rule, two factors that are extremely unreliable. In general, a ruler of this kind is neither capable of maintaining nor successful in maintaining his position. He is not capable, because unless he is a man of the greatest intelligence and skill, he cannot be expected, as a mere former private citizen, to know how to command; and he is not able to maintain his position because he does not have loyal forces that will support him. Furthermore, states that spring up suddenly, like all things in nature that sprout and grow quickly, cannot develop the necessary roots and connections, and hence they expire with the first bad weather. As I have

---

24. Darius I (550–486 BCE), King of Persia, also known as Darius the Great, attempted to conquer Greece but was ultimately defeated by the Athenians at Marathon in 490 BCE.

mentioned, the only exceptions are princes who, though they have become princes suddenly, have so much skill that they instantly know how to use and conserve what Fortune has dropped in their laps. Once they have their principality, they are quick to lay the foundations that others have had to lay before becoming princes.

I would like to illustrate with two examples from our recent history the two ways – by skill or by Fortune – of becoming prince: those of Francesco Sforza and Cesare Borgia. Sforza, through well-chosen means and great skill, began as a private citizen and became the Duke of Milan. What he gained with a thousand toils, he maintained with little effort. On the other hand, Cesare Borgia, called Duke Valentino by the people, acquired his state through his father's good fortune, and through his father's subsequent bad fortune lost it; this though Borgia used every means in his power and did all that a prudent and skilful man must do in order to establish himself in those states which the arms and good fortune of another have granted him. Because, as I have already stated, he who does not lay foundations first, must do so with prodigious skill later, even if this entails hardship for the architect and danger to the edifice. If one considers the system that Cesare Borgia applied, it is clear that he had laid strong foundations for his future power. In my view he is an important example, as I know not what better precept to give a new prince. If in the end Borgia did not prevail, it was not his fault, but the result of the extreme malignity of Fortune.

Pope Alexander VI wanted to make his son Cesare Borgia great, but he encountered many difficulties. He could not find a way of making him prince of a state that did not belong to the Church, and he knew that if he attempted to give his son a state that did belong to the Church, the Duke of Milan and the Venetians would intervene; Faenza and Rimini already stood under the protection of Venice. Furthermore, the Italian mercenary armies, particularly those the pope would most need, were in the hands of rulers who had reason to fear his growing power. He could not trust them, as they all belonged to the Orsini and Colonna clans and their allies. He had to disrupt the existing order and create turmoil in those rulers' states in order to gain control of part of them. This proved easy enough, because he found that the Venetians, for their own motives, intended to bring the French back into Italy. Not only did the pope not oppose this, but he facilitated it by obliging King Louis with an annulment of his former marriage. So Louis entered Italy with the help of the Venetians and the blessing of the pope, and no sooner had Louis set foot in Milan than he supplied the pope with men for the latter's campaign in the Romagna, which the pope conquered unhindered as he had the support and backing of the king.[25]

So after Cesare Borgia had acquired the Romagna and defeated the Colonna family, he intended to maintain the Romagna and expand further. But Borgia faced two impediments: his army, which did not seem loyal, and the designs of France. He sensed that the army of the Orsini, which he had been using, could not be relied upon. He feared that it would not only interfere with his further conquests, but take from him what he had already acquired, and that the King of France would follow suit. Borgia was confirmed in this when, after the conquest of Faenza, he attacked Bologna and saw how half-heartedly the Orsini went into battle. King Louis's intentions also became clear when Borgia attacked Tuscany after successfully taking the Duchy of Urbino, and Louis forced him to retreat. Consequently, Borgia decided to depend no longer on the army and goodwill of another. The first thing he did was to weaken the Orsini and Colonna factions in Rome by winning over all the noblemen who supported them, making them his own noblemen and granting them large stipends. He bestowed upon them, according to their rank, army commands and government positions. The result was that within a few months their affection for their former leaders was transferred to Borgia. He now waited for an opportunity to destroy the Orsini, having already dispersed the house of Colonna. An excellent opportunity presented itself, and he made excellent use of it. The Orsini had realized too late that the power of Borgia and the Church meant their ruin; they assembled at Magione, in Perugino, and fomented rebellions in Urbino and throughout the Romagna, which put Borgia in a very precarious position. He managed to overcome these dangers with the help of the French, but once he regained power, he did not trust France or any other outside force. So that he would not have to put their allegiance to him to the test, he turned to deception. He was such a master of dissimulation that the Orsini, through the mediation of Signor Paolo Orsini, were prepared to reach a reconciliation. Borgia showered

---

25. Pope Alexander's son, Cesare Borgia, was appointed commander of the papal armies.

Paolo Orsini with every courtesy in order to reassure him, giving him money, precious garments, and horses. Then Borgia set a trap for the Orsini at Sinigallia, and they foolishly walked right into it. By eliminating the leaders and turning their followers into his allies, Borgia laid a solid foundation for his power, having the whole of the Romagna and the Duchy of Urbino in his grip. What is more important, it was clear that he had gained the friendship of the Romagna and all its people, who had begun to experience the benefits of his rule.

I would also like to mention the following, because it is noteworthy and merits imitation: When Cesare Borgia took over the Romagna, he found it to have been ruled by weak princes who would sooner rob their subjects than govern them, causing dissension rather than unity. Robbery, intrigue, and every kind of evil had been rampant throughout the province, and Borgia found it essential to set up a strong government in order to pacify it and make it submit to his rule. He put in charge a resolute and ruthless man, Ramiro de Lorqua, giving him complete authority, and within the shortest time de Lorqua brought peace and unity to the Romagna, gaining much power and influence in the process. But Borgia judged that such excessive authority over the people could have dangerous consequences, as it might arouse their hatred, so he set up a civil court in the centre of the province, with an excellent presiding judge, every city having its own advocate. Borgia was aware that de Lorqua's rigour had created hatred among the people, and in order to purge their minds and win them over, he decided to make it clear that if there had been any cruelty it had been triggered by his minister's abrasive nature. At the first opportunity, he had de Lorqua cut in two on the main square in Cesena, with a piece of wood and a bloody knife at his side. The brutality of this spectacle left the people both stunned and appeased.

But to return from our digression. Cesare Borgia now found himself powerful and to some extent secure, being well armed and having to a great extent destroyed neighbouring armies that might have put him in harm's way. If he wanted to continue expanding his acquisitions, he now had to take the King of France into account. For Borgia knew that Louis, who had realized his mistake too late, would not allow him to expand his territories. So Borgia began seeking new allies, and vacillating with France in its campaign against the Kingdom of Naples and the Spaniards who were besieging Gaeta.[26] His intention was to secure himself against the French, which he could have done with ease had Pope Alexander lived. This was how Borgia handled the problems at hand. As for his future problems, his main fear was that the next pope might be ill disposed towards him and attempt to take away what Pope Alexander had given him.

Cesare Borgia set out to secure his position vis-à-vis the Church in four ways: First, to extinguish the bloodlines of the lords he had dispossessed, in order to take away a future pope's opportunity of using them; second, to win over all the noblemen of Rome, in order to keep the pope in check; third, to gain as much influence as he could within the College of Cardinals; and fourth, to acquire as large an empire as possible before Pope Alexander died so that he could resist an initial attack from any enemy without assistance from others. Of these four schemes, he had accomplished only three by the time Pope Alexander died;[27] the fourth he had almost achieved. He had killed as many of the lords he had dispossessed as he could get his hands on (only a few managed to escape), he won over the Roman noblemen, and he controlled the largest faction in the College of Cardinals. As for his further conquests, he already owned Perugia and Piombino, held Pisa under his protection, and had designs on Tuscany. As he no longer had to defer to France (the Spaniards had already robbed France of the Kingdom of Naples, with the result that both the French and the Spaniards were compelled to buy Borgia's friendship), he would have conquered Pisa. After this, Lucca and Siena would have been quick to capitulate, partly out of fear and partly to spite the Florentines, and the Florentines could have done nothing about it. Had Borgia succeeded – and he was on the point of success the very year Pope Alexander died – he would have amassed so many forces and so much influence that he could have imposed his own will, depending on his own power and skill and not on the Fortune or arms of others.

But Pope Alexander died five years after Borgia had first drawn his

26. Naples was claimed by the French king Charles VIII, who held it briefly in 1495, but it was taken by the Spanish in 1503. Borgia had initially supported the French claim, but by 1503 proved to be 'vacillating' in his support when he did not send troops as expected to help the town of Gaeta, which the Spanish army was besieging.
27. August 18, 1504.

sword, leaving him with nothing secured but the province of the Romagna (all the other possessions being up in the air). Borgia was now caught between two powerful enemy armies, and deathly ill. But he had great ferocity and skill, and was acutely aware of how men were to be won or lost. The foundations he had laid in such a short time were so sturdy that he could have stood firm against any difficulty, if [the French and Spanish] armies had not been bearing down on him and had he not been so very ill. The sturdiness of these foundations was clear, for his province waited more than a month for him. In Rome, although barely alive, he remained secure. And though the Ballioni, Vitelli, and Orsini came to Rome, they could not raise a following against him. Even if Borgia could not dictate the selection of the new pope, at least he managed to prevent a choice of which he did not approve. Had he not been ill when Pope Alexander died, he would have had no difficulty. Borgia himself told me on the day Pope Julius II was elected that he, Borgia, had carefully weighed everything that might happen after his father, Pope Alexander, died, and had found a solution for everything. There was only one thing he had not anticipated: the possibility that he himself might be at death's door.

Having laid out all the actions Borgia took, I can find nothing to reproach him with. I would even say, as I already have, that he serves as an excellent example of a prince who rose to power through Fortune and by means of the arms of others. He had great courage and lofty aspirations, and could not have conducted himself in any other way. The only things that foiled his designs were the brevity of Pope Alexander's life and his own illness. Hence, a prince wishing to secure himself against enemies in his new principality cannot find a more compelling example than Cesare Borgia of how to gain friends, how to win by force or deception, how to make the populace love and fear him, how to gain the loyalty and respect of his soldiers, the necessity of eliminating those who can or will harm him, and the importance of substituting new laws for old. Borgia was exemplary in both his severity and his kindness. He was magnanimous and liberal, eliminated disloyal troops and marshalled new ones, and cultivated friendships with kings and princes so that they had to either help him with favours or confront him with caution. Borgia's only error was to allow Julius to become the next pope. This was a bad decision because, as I have already stated, even if he could not make the man he wanted pope, he could at least have prevented the accession of a pope he did not want. He should never have agreed to the papacy of any of the cardinals he had harmed, or who would have cause to fear him once they became pope, since men will attack you out of fear or hatred. Among the men Borgia had harmed were San Piero ad Vincula,[28] Colonna, San Giorgio, and Ascanio. All the other claimants to the papacy would have had to fear him, except for Rouen and the Spaniards – Rouen because of his connection to the King of France, the Spaniards because of kinship and obligation. Therefore, Borgia's first choice for pope should have been a Spaniard, and if not a Spaniard, then Rouen. But he should not have chosen San Piero ad Vincula. For whoever believes that great advancement and new benefits make men forget old injuries is mistaken. Hence Borgia made a bad decision. And it was this decision that ultimately brought about his ruin.

28. Pope Julius II, who was Cardinal of San Piero ad Vincula before being elected to the pontificate.

CHAPTER EIGHT

OF THOSE WHO BECOME
PRINCES THROUGH EVIL

I must mention two other ways for a private citizen to become a prince that cannot be attributed to Fortune or skill, though I shall discuss one of them at greater length when I speak of republics. These are when a man obtains a principality in an evil or nefarious way, or when a private citizen, by the favour of his fellow citizens, becomes the prince of his state. Speaking of the first way, I shall offer two examples, one ancient, the other from our times, and shall leave it at that, as these examples will be enough for anyone constrained to imitate them.

When Agathocles the Sicilian became King of Syracuse, he did so not only as a private citizen, but as one who came from the lowliest and most humble circumstances. He was the son of a potter, and led a wicked life from first to last.[29] And yet he combined his wickedness with such skill of mind and body that when he joined the army, he rose through the ranks to become Praetor of Syracuse. Once established in that position, he set about becoming prince and retaining his principality by means of violence, without depending ón others for that

29. Justin writes in *Epitome of the Philippic History of Pompeius Trogus*, Book XXII, chapter 1: '[Agathocles] rose to royal power from a birth that was humble and base. In fact, he was born in Sicily to a potter. His youth was no more honourable than his birth, for being remarkable for his beauty and physical charm, he lived for a long time by submitting himself to being ravished. Emerging from puberty, he transferred his lust from men to women. Having thus become notorious with both sexes, he changed his way of life to that of a mercenary.'

which he had originally been granted by his fellow citizens. He conspired with Hamilcar the Carthaginian,[30] who was waging war in Sicily with his army, and one morning Agathocles called together the people and the senate of Syracuse as if to discuss important issues concerning the republic, and then at a signal to his soldiers had them kill all the senators and the richest men of the city.[31] Then he became the unchallenged prince of that city. And though the Carthaginians defeated him twice and finally besieged Syracuse, he managed to defend the city, and, leaving a part of his army to withstand the siege, left on a campaign with the rest to assault Africa. Within a short time he freed Syracuse from the siege and brought Carthage to its knees, forcing it to reach an agreement with him and to content itself with the possession of Africa, leaving Sicily to Agathocles.

If one weighs Agathocles's actions and skill, there is not much that can be attributed to Fortune. As I have pointed out, he did not gain his principality through anyone's favour, but rose to it through the ranks of the army with a thousand privations and dangers, and then kept possession of the principality through many bold and dangerous feats. And yet we cannot define as skilful killing one's fellow citizens, betraying one's friends, and showing no loyalty, mercy, or moral obligation. These means can lead to power, but not glory. Because if one considers Agathocles's skill at plunging into and out of danger, and the greatness of his spirit in enduring and overcoming adversity, he cannot be judged inferior to the most excellent leaders. In other words, one cannot attribute to Fortune or skill what he attained without either of them.

In our own times, during the reign of Pope Alexander VI, we have the example of Oliverotto da Fermo. He had been orphaned as a child and raised by his maternal uncle, Giovanni Fogliani, and in his early years had been sent to serve under Paolo Vitelli to master the military

30. A Carthaginian general fighting in Sicily, not to be confused with Hannibal's father, Hamilcar (d. 229 BCE), also a general in Sicily.
31. Justin writes in *Epitome of the Philippic History of Pompeius Trogus,* Book XXII, chapter 2: 'Having received from him [Hamilcar] five thousand African soldiers, he put to death the most powerful among the foremost citizens. Then he ordered the populace to assemble in the theatre, feigning that he wished to redraw the constitution of the state, also calling together the senate in the Gymnasium, under the guise of laying the groundwork. Having set this up, he sent his troops to besiege the people, had all the senators slaughtered, and then proceeded to kill all the wealthiest and most prominent plebeians.'

arts, so that he might attain a high rank in the army. When Paolo died, Oliverotto fought under Paolo's brother Vitellozzo, and very quickly, being resourceful and vigorous in body and mind, became commander of Vitellozzo's army. But he felt that serving under others was unbecoming. He decided to seize the town of Fermo with the support of Vitellozzo and the help of some of Fermo's citizens, who preferred servitude to freedom for their city. Oliverotto wrote to his uncle Giovanni Fogliani that, having been away from home for many years, he wanted to return to see him and his town and reacquaint himself with his patrimony. He wrote that in all these years he had fought in order to acquire honour, and now he wanted his fellow citizens to see that he had not spent his time in vain. He wanted to return with honour, accompanied by a hundred friends and servants on horseback, and asked his uncle to ensure that the citizens of Fermo would receive him with ceremony, which would also reflect well on his uncle as his guardian. And Giovanni did not fail to show his nephew every courtesy. Having him received with honour by the citizens of Fermo, he quartered him and his men in his houses. After a few days, having waited to put into place what was necessary for his future wickedness, Oliverotto ordered a great feast, to which he invited Giovanni Fogliani and all the foremost men of Fermo. After the courses had been eaten and the usual entertainments were over, Oliverotto artfully introduced delicate subjects, speaking of the greatness of Pope Alexander and his son Cesare and of their campaigns. Giovanni and the others responded, and Oliverotto suggested that such delicate matters should be discussed in a more private place. He retired to a chamber with Giovanni and the other citizens, and no sooner had they seated themselves than soldiers emerged from a hiding place and slaughtered Giovanni and the rest. After the slaughter, Oliverotto mounted a horse and took over the town, besieging the supreme magistrate in his palace. The citizens were forced to obey him out of fear, and he made them form a new government with himself as prince. As everyone who would have opposed him was dead, they could not harm him, and Oliverotto reinforced his position with new civil and military laws. Within a year, he was secure in the town of Fermo and had become a source of fear for its neighbours. It would have been as hard to defeat him as to defeat Agathocles, had Oliverotto not let himself be deceived by Cesare Borgia, who, as I have mentioned, trapped the Orsini and the Vitelli in Sinigallia. It was in Sinigallia, a year after Oliverotto had murdered his uncle, that he was strangled along with Vitellozzo, who had been his tutor in skill and wickedness.

One might wonder how Agathocles and others like him, after countless betrayals and so much cruelty, could live so long and securely in their states and defend themselves from outside enemies, and why they were never conspired against by their citizens, whereas many others could not retain their states through cruelty, either in times of peace or in the uncertain times of war. I believe this depends upon whether cruelty is used well or badly. Cruelty can be called well used (if it is even permitted to use the word 'well' in connection with evil) if it is executed at a single stroke out of the necessity to secure one's power, and is then not continued but converted into the greatest possible benefit for one's subjects. Badly used cruelty is cruelty that, even if initially limited, increases with time rather than subsiding. Those who follow the first path can maintain their position in their state with the blessing of God and man, as Agathocles did. The others cannot possibly survive.

A prince can conclude from this that when he conquers a state, he must weigh all the acts of cruelty that are necessary, and execute them all at a single stroke so they will not have to be repeated every day, and by not repeating them assure the people and win them over by subsequently benefiting them. Whoever proceeds otherwise, through fear or bad judgment, must always keep a knife at hand. He can never rely on his subjects, as they cannot feel secure under him. Therefore any cruelty has to be executed at once, so that the less it is tasted, the less it offends; while benefits must be dispensed little by little, so that they will be savoured all the more. Primarily, a prince must live with his subjects in such a way that no incident, either good or bad, should make him change his course, because when bad times cause him to employ more stringent methods, it will be too late, nor will the good he does benefit him, because it will be judged to have been forced.

CHAPTER NINE

OF THE CIVIL PRINCIPALITY

But let us consider the other alternative, when a private citizen becomes prince of his native state through the favour of his fellow citizens, and not through wickedness or some violence that proves intolerable to the citizens. Such a principality can be called a civil principality, since to acquire it the prince does not have to depend entirely on skill or Fortune, but rather on a fortunate astuteness. One acquires this principality through the favour of either the people or the nobles, because in every city there are two opposing humours. This arises from the fact that the nobles want to command and oppress the people, but the people do not want to be commanded or oppressed by the nobles.[32] These two opposing impulses within a city will result in one of three outcomes: a principality, liberty, or anarchy.

The principality is brought about by the people or the nobility, depending on which has the opportunity. When the nobles see that they cannot stand up to the people, they put all their support behind one of their own, making him prince so they can satisfy their ambition in the safety of his shadow. And the people, finding that they cannot stand up to the nobility, put all their support behind one man and make him prince, in the hope that his authority will shield them.

32. Machiavelli writes in *Discourses,* Book I, chapter 5: 'For without doubt, if one considers the respective aims of the nobles and the populace, one sees in the former a strong desire to dominate, and in the latter merely a desire not to be dominated.'

A prince who obtains a state with the help of the people maintains his position with less difficulty than a prince who acquires it with the help of the nobility, because in the latter case he is surrounded by men who consider themselves his equals and whom he therefore cannot command or govern as he pleases. But a prince who acquires a principality through the favour of the people is unhampered: Only a few in his circle are unready to obey him. Furthermore, one cannot satisfy the nobles in a manner that is just and does not harm the people, but one can so satisfy the people, because their aspirations are more just than those of the nobles: The nobles want to oppress them, but the people want only not to be oppressed. Moreover, a prince cannot shield himself against a populace that is hostile toward him, because there are too many of them; but he can shield himself against the nobles, as they are few in number.[33] The worst that a prince can expect from a hostile populace is for them to abandon him, but from hostile noblemen he has also to fear their conspiring against him. Noblemen, having more foresight and cunning, tend to act in time to save themselves, and are quick to seek out those who they hope will prevail. The prince is constrained always to live with that same populace, but he can do well enough without those same noblemen, as he is able to make and unmake them at will, giving and taking away their power as he pleases.

To clarify this point, I propose that noblemen must be considered in two ways: Either they link themselves entirely to your destiny, or they do not. Those who link themselves to you and are not greedy should be honoured and loved. Those who do not are acting out of pusillanimity and a natural lack of courage. You should make use of those among them who offer good counsel, because in prosperity they will bring you honour, while in difficult times you need not fear them. But if out of malicious design and ambition they do not align themselves with you, it is a sign that they are thinking more of themselves than of you. A prince must be on his guard against them. He should fear them as if they were declared enemies, because in adversity they will inevitably help to bring about his ruin.

---

33. Machiavelli writes in *Discourses*, Book I, chapter 16: 'In fact, I consider those princes unfortunate who are compelled to resort to exceptional means to secure their state because the populace is their enemy, for he who has as his enemy the few can secure himself easily and without much turmoil, but he who has the whole populace as his enemy can never secure himself.'

And yet he who becomes prince through the favour of the people must keep the people on his side. This should be simple enough, as all they ask of him is that he not oppress them. But he who becomes prince through the favour of the nobility against the will of the people must make it a priority to win over the people, which is easy enough if he becomes their protector. Because men, when they encounter benevolence where they expected harm, show greater gratitude to their benefactor, and the populace becomes even more supportive than if the prince had acquired the state through their favour. And the prince can earn this favour in many ways, but as these vary greatly depending on the circumstances, one cannot lay down a fixed rule. I will only conclude that a prince must have the people on his side, otherwise he will not have support in adverse times.

Prince Nabis of Sparta fended off a siege led by the whole of Greece and an illustrious Roman army, managing to save the state and city of his birth.[34] He overcame the danger, having to protect himself against only a few of his subjects, an endeavour that would have failed had the populace been against him.

And let nobody respond with the trite proverb that he who builds upon the masses builds upon sand, because this proverb holds only when a private citizen builds a foundation on the populace in the hope that they will come to his rescue when he is in trouble with magistrates or his enemies. In this case he might find himself disabused, as were the Gracchi in Rome and Giorgio Scali in Florence.[35]

But if a prince builds a foundation on the populace and can command, and is a man of courage unruffled in adversity who has taken his precautions, a man who has made himself popular with the people

34. Nabis (d. 192 BCE), the last king of an independent Sparta, managed to maintain his power despite the wars between Rome and Philip V of Macedon and their allies that were destabilizing the territories of all the Greek states.

35. The Gracchi brothers were influential Roman statesmen whose reforms acted as a catalyst to end the Roman Republic. Giorgio Scali was one of the Florentine political figures who came to power after the popular Revolt of the Ciompi in 1378. Machiavelli writes in *Florentine Histories* (Book III, chapter 21) that as Scali was being executed by the populace he had championed, he 'blamed himself for having set too much stock in the populace, which can be moved and corrupted by every voice, every act, every suspicion.' The fifteenth-century chronicler Piero Vagliente attributed to Giorgio Scali the 'trite proverb' that Machiavelli quotes: 'Giorgio Scali, who said that he who builds upon deferring to the masses builds upon shit.'

through his spirit and government, he will never be abandoned by the populace. Principalities tend to be vulnerable when they move from civil to absolute order, because princes command either directly or through magistrates. In the latter case, the prince finds his position weaker and more dangerous because he is at the mercy of citizens who have become magistrates. They can, particularly in adverse times, easily take the state away from him, either by abandoning him or by opposing him. Once this happens, the prince no longer has time to establish his absolute authority, because the populace are used to following the orders of the magistrates, and will not obey the prince's orders during difficult times. In adversity, he will find that there is a lack of people he can trust, because a prince in his position cannot rely on his experience during times of peace, when citizens are in need of the state and fall all over each other with promises, eagerly proclaiming that they are willing to die for him when death is at a safe distance. But in adverse times, when the state needs its citizens, only a few are to be found. This experience is all the more dangerous in that it can be experienced only once. Therefore, a wise prince must find a way in which his citizens will consider him and the state to be indispensable in every circumstance and at all times. Then his citizens will be always faithful.

CHAPTER TEN

HOW THE STRENGTH OF
PRINCIPALITIES IS TO BE MEASURED

In examining the characteristics of all these types of principalities I have mentioned, it is important to keep another consideration in mind: whether a prince rules a state strong enough to enable him to stand on his own or whether he will always need the protection of others. To clarify this point, I judge a prince capable of standing on his own when he has enough men or money to gather an army capable of engaging in battle anyone who comes to attack him; and I judge a prince as needing the assistance of others when he is not strong enough to engage an enemy on the battlefield and is compelled to seek refuge behind his walls, which he then has to defend. I have already discussed the first case and will discuss it further;[36] as for the second, one can only urge such a prince to stock up on provisions and fortify his city but disregard the surrounding area. Whoever sufficiently fortifies his city and has looked after his subjects (which I have already touched on and will do so again later),[37] will not be attacked without great hesitation, because men are always wary of enterprises in which the difficulties are obvious. And it is quite clear that attacking a prince whose

36. See chapter 6 and chapters 12–14.
37. Machiavelli touched on this matter in the previous chapter when he discussed the importance of 'the favour of the people' to the prince. He makes mention of it again in the following chapters.

city is well fortified and who is not hated by his people is not an easy matter.

The cities of Germany are very free. They own but little of the land that surrounds them, obey the emperor when it suits them, and fear neither him nor any neighbouring king. This is because they are well enough fortified so that anyone who intends to invade them would see it as a strenuous and difficult endeavour, as the cities have enough ditches and walls and sufficient artillery and keep themselves stocked with a year's supply of food, drink, and firewood. Furthermore, these cities have the means of keeping their citizens fed by providing them with enough work for a year, occupying them in activities that are the lifeblood of the city and that yield the products that sustain the people. In this way, municipal funds are not depleted either. The German cities also hold military exercises in high esteem and have many ordinances that maintain them.

Therefore a prince who has organized his city in this way and has not given his people cause to hate him will not be attacked. (And if he should be, the enemy will withdraw in shame, because the affairs of this world are so changeable that one cannot sit idly and wait outside a city with a besieging army.) Some might argue that the populace could lose heart if it sees its possessions outside the walls in flames, and that a long siege and self-interest will result in the people's forgetting their love for their prince. To this I reply that a prudent and spirited prince can overcome these difficulties. At times he must inspire his people with the hope that the evil will be short-lived; at other times he must instil in them a fear of the enemy's cruelty and, when necessary, cleverly shield himself from those individuals among his subjects who might pose a threat. It is also to be expected that the enemy, as soon as it appears, will ravage and burn the area outside the city at a time when the populace is still ardent to defend itself. Therefore the prince should not hesitate, because within a few days, once the people's spirits have flagged, the harm will have been done, the wounds inflicted, and it will be too late for remedy.

The populace will have all the more reason to unite behind their prince when they see that he is obligated to them, as their houses have been burned and their possessions ruined in his defence. (It is man's nature to obligate himself as much for the benefits he gives as for the benefits he receives.) Therefore, all things considered, it is not difficult for a prudent prince to bolster the spirits of his people throughout a siege as long as there is no lack of provisions or ammunition.

CHAPTER ELEVEN

OF ECCLESIASTICAL PRINCIPALITIES

All that remains now is to consider ecclesiastical principalities. The difficulties they present all occur before they are acquired, for while they are acquired either by skill or by Fortune, they are maintained without the one or the other. This is because ecclesiastical principalities are sustained by age-old religious institutions, which are so strong and efficacious that these principalities will maintain their princes in power regardless of how they live or what they do. Their princes are the only ones who have states they do not defend, and subjects they do not govern. Although such states are undefended, they are not taken away from these princes, and the subjects, although they are ungoverned, remain unconcerned, and neither think of, nor are able to estrange themselves from, these princes. Thus these are the only principalities that are secure and successful. But since they are under the guidance of a superior power that the mind of man cannot fathom, I will not discuss them. For, as they are exalted and maintained by God, it would be the act of a presumptuous and audacious man to do so. Nevertheless, one might ask how it is that the Church has gained so much temporal power, since up to the time of Pope Alexander VI, Italian rulers (and here I include every baron and lord, however minor) had little regard for the pope's temporal power, though now, even the King of France trembles before it since it managed to expel him from

Italy and ruin the Venetians. In this sense, it does not seem to me redundant to commit the essentials of this situation to memory.

Italy, before King Charles of France[38] arrived, was under the power of the pope, the Venetians, the King of Naples, the Duke of Milan, and the Florentines. These rulers had two primary concerns: to prevent a foreigner from entering Italy with an army, and to prevent any single ruler among them from growing in strength by occupying more states. The pope and the Venetians worried the others most. In order to keep the Venetians in check, all the other rulers united (as happened in the defence of Ferrara),[39] and to keep the pope in check, they manipulated the barons of Rome, who were divided into the Orsini and Colonna factions, which were always fighting each other. Eyeing the pope with weapons drawn, they kept him weak and on unsteady ground. From time to time a spirited pope did emerge – like Sixtus IV – but neither Fortune nor ingenuity could free him from these warring factions. The brevity of a pope's tenure in office was also a factor, because in the ten years that his pontificate might last, he could not be expected to subdue either faction. If, for instance, one pope managed to crush the Colonna, another pope, who might be an enemy of the Orsini, would see to it that the Colonna resurged, but he in turn would not hold office long enough to see the Orsini crushed. As a result, the pope's temporal power was not held in high esteem in Italy.

Then came Pope Alexander VI, who of all the popes in history demonstrated the extent to which a pope could succeed with the help of money and arms. By way of his son, Cesare Borgia, and the invasion of the French, Alexander did all the things I have already discussed.[40] And though his intent was to make Cesare Borgia great and not the Church, his actions ultimately resulted in the greatness of the Church, which, after his and Cesare's deaths, became the beneficiary of all his efforts. Then came Pope Julius. He found the Church powerful and in possession of the whole of the Romagna, with the barons of Rome destroyed and their factions crushed by Pope Alexander. He also found the way open to accumulating money in ways that had never before

38. Charles VIII invaded Italy in 1494.
39. Duke Ercole d'Este of Ferrara fought an alliance of the Republic of Venice and Pope Sixtus IV from 1482 to 1484.
40. See chapter 7.

been possible. Pope Julius not only took advantage of these opportunities but added to them. He set out to gain Bologna, destroy the Venetians, and drive the French out of Italy. In all this he succeeded, and he is worthy of even more praise since he did everything in order to strengthen the Church and not any of his own people. He also kept the Orsini and Colonna factions in the weakened condition in which he found them. Though there were leaders among these families ready to cause trouble, two factors kept them in check: the power of the Church, and the fact that they no longer had any cardinals in the College of Cardinals, which is where many of the troubles in the past had begun. Neither faction would have remained subdued had they had their cardinals in place, because it is these cardinals who incite the different factions, and the barons of the Orsini and the Colonna families are then forced to defend themselves. It is from the ambitions of the prelates of the Church that discord and tumult has always arisen among the barons.

Hence, His Holiness Pope Leo has found the pontificate in a most powerful condition, which leads one to hope that whereas the other popes made it great with the help of arms, he will make it even greater and more revered through his goodness and his many other virtues.

CHAPTER TWELVE

OF THE DIFFERENT TYPES OF ARMIES,
AND OF MERCENARIES

I have now laid out in detail all the qualities of the principalities that I proposed to discuss at the beginning of this work; I have weighed the reasons for their successes and failures and shown the ways in which many men tried to acquire and keep these principalities. It remains for me to discuss the means of attack and defence that can be applied to each of the previously mentioned cases.

We have already discussed how a prince needs a good foundation[41] if he wants to avoid failure. The primary foundation of all states – new, old, or mixed – is good laws and a good army. And as there cannot be good laws where there is not a good army, and where there is a good army there have to be good laws, I will omit any discussion of laws and speak only of armies.

The army with which a prince defends his state is either his own, a mercenary army, an auxiliary army,[42] or one that is a mix of these. The mercenary and auxiliary armies are useless and dangerous. A prince who holds a state that is founded on the strength of mercenary armies will never be firm or secure, since such armies are divided, ambitious, without discipline and fickle – brave in the face of friends, cowardly in

---

41. Chapters 7 and 9.
42. As Machiavelli explains in *Discourses*, Book II, chapter 20: 'Auxiliary troops are those which another prince or republic sends to help you, and which are paid and commanded by them.'

the face of enemies. Such soldiers have neither fear of God nor dependability with men, and one's ruin can be held off only as long as an assault can be deferred. In peace one is despoiled by the mercenaries, in war by one's enemies. The reason for this is that all that keeps mercenaries on the battlefield are the negligible wages you pay them, which are not sufficient to make them want to die for you. They are eager to be your soldiers as long as you are not at war. The moment there is a war, they either take flight or desert. It is easy enough for me to make my case since the present ruin of Italy has been brought about by a reliance on mercenary armies over a period of many years.[43] There have been mercenaries who were effective and did well fighting other mercenaries, but as soon as foreign forces invaded, they showed their true colours. As a result, King Charles of France was able to conquer Italy with a piece of chalk,[44] and he who said that our sins were responsible was speaking the truth,[45] though they were not the sins that he had in mind but the ones I have laid out. As these were sins committed by the Italian princes, it was they who had to pay the price.

I would like to demonstrate more fully the inadequacy of mercenary armies. Mercenary generals are either excellent or not. If they are, one cannot rely on them because they will inevitably aspire to their own greatness, either by oppressing the prince they are working for, or by oppressing others whom the prince does not intend to oppress. If the mercenary general is not adroit, he will ruin the prince by losing his battles. If someone were to argue that this is true regardless of whose hand – mercenary or not – carries the weapon, I maintain that the weapons must be wielded by a prince or by a republic. The prince should personally take on the role of general.[46] The republic

---

43. Machiavelli was writing during the period of the Italian Wars, which had begun in 1494 with the invasion of Charles VIII of France. All sides relied heavily on foreign mercenaries.

44. Philippe de Commynes (1447–1511), a noted historian and diplomat of the French court, wrote in *Mémoirs* (Book VII, chapter 14): 'As Pope Alexander who reigns today has said, "The French have come with wooden spurs, their quartermasters, quite unhindered, carrying bits of chalk to mark the doors of houses where they are to be quartered." '

45. Machiavelli is referring to Savonarola, who in his fiery sermons blamed the affliction of Florence on the Florentines' luxuriant ways.

46. Machiavelli's *Discourses*, Book I, chapter 30, opens with the line: 'To escape the need of living in constant suspicion or being ungrateful, a prince must himself go out on military expeditions, as the Roman emperors initially did and as the Turk does in our times.'

should send out one of its citizens as general, and if he does not turn out to be valiant, he must be replaced. If he is valiant, he must be held in check by laws that do not let him overstep the mark. Experience has shown that only princes and republics that have their own army make great progress, while mercenary armies do nothing but harm. A republic that has its own army is much less likely to come under the sway of one of its own citizens than one that relies on foreign mercenaries.

Both Rome and Sparta were for many centuries armed and free. The Swiss are well armed and very free. As for mercenary armies in ancient times, we have the example of the Carthaginians, who were almost overwhelmed by their mercenary soldiers after the first war with the Romans, even though the Carthaginians had their own citizens as generals. The Thebans had made Philip of Macedon their general after the death of Epaminondas, but once Philip was victorious in battle he took away the Thebans' liberty.[47] The Milanese, after the death of Duke Filippo Visconti, hired Francesco Sforza to fight the Venetians: After Sforza vanquished them at Caravaggio he joined the Venetians to oppress the Milanese, his patrons. Francesco Sforza's father, a mercenary to Queen Giovanna of Naples, left her defenceless, and she was forced to throw herself on the mercy of the King of Aragon so as not to lose her realm.

In the past the Venetians and the Florentines managed to expand their empires with the help of mercenaries, and the mercenary generals did not make themselves princes but stood by them. This, however, in the case of the Florentines was only because they were favoured by Fortune. They had employed some illustrious generals whom they had cause to fear, but some of these happened to lose battles, others ran into staunch opposition, and still others turned their ambitions elsewhere. Giovanni Aucut was one of the mercenary generals who did not win, so we do not know where his loyalty would ultimately have lain.[48] But it will be admitted that had he been victorious, the Florentines would have been at his mercy. Francesco Sforza always had the Braccio faction against him – each side watching the other. Sforza turned

---

47. Epaminondas (c. 410–362 BCE) was a Theban statesman and general who made Thebes the foremost military power in Greece from 370 to 362 BCE. After his death, Thebes declined into civil strife, and in 346 was forced to admit Philip of Macedon's garrisons.
48. The English condottiere Sir John Hawkwood.

his ambition to Lombardy, and Braccio marched against the Church and the Kingdom of Naples.

But let us consider our times. The Florentines hired as their general Paolo Vitelli, a most astute man who had risen from private citizen to a position of great prominence. Had he conquered Pisa for them, the Florentines would have been forced to keep him, for they would have been in grave danger had he gone over to the Pisans. But had the Florentines kept him, they would have ended up under his thumb.

In the case of the Venetians, if one weighs their successes it is clear that they acted wisely and bravely as long as they used their own soldiers to fight their wars, which they did before they began to expand from Venice onto the mainland. Both their noblemen and armed plebeians had always fought most valiantly. But the moment the Venetians stepped on terra firma they lost their skill and resorted to mercenaries, as was common throughout Italy. At the beginning of their expansion they had a small state but a substantial reputation, and so did not have much to fear from their mercenary generals. But as they expanded, which they did under General Carmignola, they received ample proof of their error.[49] Carmignola had shown his skill in battle, having defeated the Duke of Milan, but subsequently the Venetians saw his ardour for battle cool. They saw that they could not expect any further victories from him but were not willing or able to relieve him of his duties, since they did not want to lose what they had gained if he switched allegiance. So for their own security they were compelled to execute him. After Carmignola, the Venetians hired mercenaries like Bartolomeo da Bergamo, Roberto da San Severino, and the Count of Pitigliano, from whom they had more reason to fear defeat than victory (as happened at the Battle of Vailà, where in one day Venice lost all that it had laboriously gained over eight hundred years). Mercenary armies afford only slow, laborious, and insubstantial victories, while the losses they bring are sudden and spectacular.

As these examples have brought me to Italy, which has been ruled for so many years by mercenary armies, I would like to discuss them in greater depth, so that by tracing their origin and development it will

49. Francesco Bussone da Carmignola, c. 1380–1432, commanded Florentine and Venetian forces against Milan. His irresolute conduct of the war led the Venetians to suspect treason, and he was tried and executed.

be easier to remedy the problem. It must be kept in mind how, in recent times since the empire was driven out of Italy and the pope has gained in temporal power, Italy has split into more states; for many of the great cities took up arms against their nobles who had been favoured by the emperor and had oppressed them, while the Church favoured the oppressed cities in order to gain temporal power. In many other cities, their own citizens became princes. As a result, Italy fell into the hands of the Church and of several republics. Since these new rulers were priests and private citizens, they knew nothing about armies and turned to foreign mercenaries. The first to give a mercenary army prominence was Alberigo da Conio from the Romagna. From his school came, among others, Braccio and Sforza, who in their day were the arbiters of Italy. After them came all the others, who up until the present day have led these mercenary armies. The result: Italy was overrun by Charles, pillaged by Louis, ravished by Ferrando, and disgraced by the Swiss.

The mercenaries moved quickly to take away the standing of the infantry and appropriate it to themselves. They did this because, not having a state of their own and living by their profession, too few soldiers would not afford them the standing they needed, while they could not support and feed as many soldiers as they did need. So they limited themselves to the cavalry, where the force was smaller and could be fed and paid. As a result, in an army of twenty thousand you could not find two thousand infantrymen. Furthermore, the mercenary generals did their utmost to keep themselves and their soldiers out of the way of fatigue and danger, and did not kill the enemy in the fray but took prisoners, and that without ransom. They did not attack cities at night, nor did those defending the cities attack the encampments outside. They did not build stockades or ditches around their camps, and they did not go on campaigns during the winter. All these things were consistent with their military conventions and, as I have pointed out, enabled them to escape fatigue and danger. They have driven Italy into slavery and disgrace.

CHAPTER THIRTEEN

THE AUXILIARY ARMY, THE CITIZEN ARMY,
AND THE ARMY THAT COMBINES THE TWO

An auxiliary army is also a worthless army. It is the kind that a power-ful figure brings with him when you call upon to help defend you. Pope Julius did this in our times. In the campaign of Ferrara, the pope witnessed the miserable performance of his mercenary army and turned to an auxiliary one, reaching an agreement with King Ferdi-nand of Spain to come to his aid with troops. Such troops can be use-ful and good in themselves, but will almost always prove harmful to him who summons them. If this army loses, he ends up dissatisfied, and if it wins, he ends up its prisoner. Even though history is full of exam-ples, I prefer to cite the contemporary example of Pope Julius II, whose decision to turn to Ferdinand of Spain for help could not have been more ill advised. The pope was so eager to gain Ferrara that he threw himself into the arms of a foreigner. But Fortune happened to be on the pope's side, and hence he was not compelled to taste the bitter fruit of his decision, for after his auxiliary army was defeated at Ravenna[50] the Swiss routed the victorious French, much to his surprise and everyone else's. The pope was not taken prisoner by the enemy, since they had fled, nor by his auxiliary troops, since his ultimate vic-

---

50. In April 1512, the French army fought a battle with the Spanish, Venetian, and papal troops outside Ravenna. The French were victorious, but were then forced by the Swiss (then the pope's main allies) to evacuate Milan. In 1513 the Swiss routed the French at No-vara.

tory had been gained not by them but by another army. The Florentines, having no army at all, had engaged ten thousand Frenchmen to conquer Pisa, which exposed them to more danger than they had ever faced before. The Emperor of Constantinople, in order to fend off his neighbours, had brought ten thousand Turks into Greece, and once the war was over these Turks did not want to leave. This was the beginning of Greece's enslavement to the Infidel.

In short, anyone ready to lose battles should avail himself of such troops, because they are far more dangerous than mercenaries. For if you use auxiliary troops the cards are stacked against you, since they are united under the command of an outsider. But for mercenary troops to harm you, even if they are victorious, takes a certain amount of time and the right opportunity. Mercenary troops are not a single body, as it is you who assemble them and pay them. An outsider whom you appoint as their commander cannot establish his authority quickly enough to do you harm. In essence, the most dangerous aspect of mercenaries is their indolence, while that of auxiliary troops is their prowess. Wise princes have always avoided auxiliary troops and relied on their own. They have preferred defeat with their own army rather than victory with that of another, judging that a victory won with another's army is not a true victory.

I shall never hesitate to cite Cesare Borgia and his actions. He entered the Romagna at the head of an auxiliary army made up entirely of Frenchmen, and with it took Imola and Forlì. But the moment he felt that this army was not reliable, he turned to mercenaries, considering them less dangerous, and hired the Orsini and the Vitelli. When he subsequently saw that they too were unreliable, disloyal, and dangerous, he destroyed them[51] and went back to using his own men. It is easy to see the difference between these types of armies, considering Cesare Borgia's standing when he had only the French, when he had the Orsini and Vitelli, and when he was self-sufficient with his own soldiers. Then his standing increased. His reputation was at its height when men saw him in every way as the master of his own army.

Though I intended to focus on recent Italian examples, I do not wish to pass over Hiero of Syracuse, as I have already mentioned

---

51. At Sinigallia in 1502. Machiavelli's essay 'How Duke Valentino Killed the Generals Who Conspired Against Him' discusses this event in more detail.

him.[52] The Syracusans had made him general of their army, and he was quick to see that the mercenary troops, much like our own Italian condottieri, were useless. As he felt that he could neither keep them nor dismiss them, he had them slashed to pieces.[53] After that, he made war using his own troops and not those of others. I also wish to cite an example from the Old Testament. David stepped forward to fight Goliath, the Philistine challenger. Saul offered him his own armour to give him courage, but no sooner had David put it on than he cast it off again, saying that he could not make use of his own strength with another's armour. He wanted to face the enemy with his own slingshot and knife. In short, the arms of another will either fall off your back, weigh you down, or hamper you.

Louis XI's father, King Charles VII, who freed France from the English[54] with the help of Fortune and his skill, recognized the importance of having his own army. He issued a decree in his kingdom to enlist an infantry and a cavalry. After him, his son Louis disbanded the infantry and began hiring Swiss mercenaries. This mistake, followed by others, has led, as we have seen, to the many dangers France has had to face. Having given power to the Swiss, Louis undermined his own, because he disbanded his infantry and made his cavalry dependent on the mercenaries' skill. And the cavalry, once accustomed to fighting alongside the Swiss, felt it could not win without them. As a result, the French cannot stand up to the Swiss, but neither are they willing to face others on the battlefield without them. Hence the French army has become mixed – in part mercenary, in part French citizens – which is still better than an army that is entirely auxiliary or mercenary, but far inferior to an army made up entirely of one's own citizens. This example should suffice, because France would have been undefeatable had King Charles's decrees been followed and developed. But

52. See chapter 6.
53. Polybius, *Histories*, Book 1, chapter 9: 'Finding the old mercenaries disaffected and seditious, he led an expedition against the barbarians who had occupied Messene. [...] But he held back his citizen cavalry and infantry at a distance and under his personal command, as if he meant to use them to attack another side, but sent the mercenaries on ahead, allowing them to be completely slaughtered by the barbarians.'
54. King Charles VII of France (1403–61) was the father of Louis XI (1423–83). King Charles drove the English out of France (with the aid of Joan of Arc), and instituted sweeping reforms in his army by a series of ordinances, improving its recruitment and efficiency.

man's scant prudence will make him relish a dish that appears delicious while it conceals poison within.

A prince who does not perceive the ills in his principality as they arise is not truly astute. Such astuteness is afforded to few. If one considers the beginning of the decline of the Roman Empire, one will find that it began when Goth mercenaries were hired. It was then that the strength of the Roman army started to flag. All the skill and valour that was sapped from the Romans went to strengthen the Goths. Thus I conclude that no principality is safe without its own army. It is entirely at the mercy of Fortune, having failed to preserve the valour that will defend it in adversity. Wise men have always held to the maxim *quod nihil sit tam infirmum aut instabile quam fama potentiae non sua vi nixa.*[55] And 'your own power' is an army composed either of your subjects, your citizens, or your dependents. Anything else constitutes a mercenary or auxiliary army. How one's army should be organized is easy to see if one weighs the four examples I have cited above[56] and if one takes into account the method by which Philip of Macedon, the father of Alexander the Great, and many republics and principalities armed themselves – a method I fully support.

---

55. An altered quotation from Tacitus's *Annales.* 13.19.1: *Nihil rerum mortalium tam instabile ac fluxum est quam fama potentiae non sua vi nixae.* (No human matter is as unstable and changeable as the reputation of power that has no support of its own.)
56. Cesare Borgia, Hiero of Syracuse, David, and Charles VII of France.

CHAPTER FOURTEEN

OF A PRINCE'S DUTIES
CONCERNING THE MILITARY

A prince must therefore have no other thought or objective, nor dedicate himself to any other art, but that of war with its rules and discipline, because this is the only art suitable for a man who commands. It is such a powerful art that it will maintain the position of one who is born a prince, but will also often raise mere private citizens to that rank. Princes who give more thought to luxury than to arms often lose their principality. In fact, the quickest way to lose a principality is to neglect the art of war, and the best way of acquiring one is to be a master in this art.[57]

Francesco Sforza, from being a private citizen, became Duke of Milan because he was armed, while his sons after him, shrinking from the hardships of military life, ended up as private citizens after having been dukes. Furthermore, being unarmed makes you, among other things, despised, which is one of the infamies from which a prince must shield himself, as I will discuss later.[58] There is no comparison between an armed man and an unarmed one. It is not reasonable to think that an armed man might be compelled to obey an unarmed one, or that an unarmed man might be safe among the armed mercenaries he has hired. The unarmed prince will always be wary of these merce-

57. See note 46 above.
58. See chapter 19.

naries, whereas they will harbor disdain for him. There is no way for them to work well together. Hence, beside the other misfortunes already mentioned, a prince who does not understand military matters will not be respected by his soldiers and cannot trust them.

The prince must therefore never shift his attention from the exercise of war, even in times of peace, and he must do this both in action and in mind. As for action, he must not only keep his troops well trained and organized, but must also himself continuously go out hunting, keeping his body accustomed to hardship, while learning the lay of the land: how the mountains rise and the valleys dip, how the plains lie, and the nature of the rivers and marshes. He must do this with the greatest application, for such knowledge is useful in two ways. First, he will familiarize himself intimately with his own country and understand how to defend it; second, with the knowledge and experience of his own terrain, he will more easily get to know any foreign terrain he might have to explore, because any hill, valley, river, plain, or marsh that exists in Tuscany will resemble those of other provinces. In short, familiarizing one with the terrain of one's own province helps to familiarize one with the terrain of other provinces as well. A prince who lacks this knowledge lacks the most essential quality in a general, because this will train him how to hunt the enemy, choose a campsite, lead troops, and direct them in the field and in besieging towns.

Among the things Prince Philopoemen of the Achaeans has been praised for by writers is that in times of peace he thought of nothing but ways of waging war.[59] When he was out riding in the country with his friends, he often stopped and reasoned with them: 'If the enemy were up in those hills and we were here with our army, who would have the advantage? How could we attack without breaking formation? If we wanted to retreat, how would we do that? If they were to retreat, how would we pursue them?' And as Prince Philopoemen and his companions rode on, he would lay out all the circumstances that could befall an army. He would listen to the opinions of the others and share

---

59. Philopoemen (c. 252–182 BCE) was a renowned general of the Achaean League, known for his innovations in Greek military tactics. Machiavelli closely follows Livy's text (Book XXXV, chapter 28): 'Philopoemen had a great talent for directing a campaign and choosing advantageous positions, which was the result of his experience acquired through much reflection in times of peace as well as war.'

his opinions with them, which he would back up with detailed explanation, his aim being that through continuous deliberations, nothing unforeseen for which he might have no remedy would ever occur in battle.

As for the exercise of the mind, a prince must read histories and study the actions of great men so he can see how they conducted themselves in war and examine the reasons for their victories and defeats, in order to imitate the former and avoid the latter. Above all, the prince must follow the example of some great man of the past, who in turn followed the example of another great man who had been praised and honoured before him, always keeping his predecessor's deeds and actions in mind. For it is said that Alexander the Great imitated Achilles, that Caesar imitated Alexander, and that Scipio imitated Cyrus. Anyone who reads Xenophon's life of Cyrus can see in Scipio's actions how much glory his imitation of Cyrus brought him, and to what extent Scipio conformed with what Xenophon wrote about Cyrus in matters of chastity, openness, humanity, and liberality.

A wise prince must observe such methods, and never remain idle in times of peace but vigorously take advantage of them so he can be ready for times of adversity, so that when Fortune changes, she will find him prepared to resist her.

CHAPTER FIFTEEN

OF THE THINGS FOR WHICH MEN,
AND PRINCES IN PARTICULAR,
ARE PRAISED OR BLAMED

It remains now to discuss what methods and measures a prince should employ with his subjects or friends. Many have written about this, and I fear I might be considered presumptuous, particularly as I intend to depart from the principles laid down by others. As my intention is to write something useful for discerning minds, I find it more fitting to seek the truth of the matter rather than imaginary conceptions. Many have imagined republics and principalities that have never been seen or heard of, because how one lives and how one ought to live are so far apart that he who spurns what is actually done for what ought to be done will achieve ruin rather than his own preservation. A man who strives to make a show of correct comportment in every circumstance can only come to ruin among so many who have other designs. Hence it is necessary for a prince who wishes to maintain his position to learn how to be able not to be good, and to use or not use this ability according to circumstances.

Casting aside imagined things about a prince, and considering only things that are true, I argue that all men, particularly princes, since they have a higher position, are judged by qualities that attract praise or blame. This is why some princes are considered generous and others miserly;[60] one is regarded as a giver, the other as a taker; one is seen

60. Machiavelli's note: 'I am using the Tuscan term *misero* here, as *avaro* (miserly) in Italian still carries the implication of someone who wishes to acquire by robbery, while we use *misero* in Tuscan to mean someone who excessively abstains from using what is his own.'

as cruel, the other as merciful; one faithless, the other faithful; one effeminate and pusillanimous, the other fierce and spirited; one humane, the other haughty; one lascivious, the other chaste; one frank, the other sly; one rigid, the other flexible; one grave, the other jovial; one religious, the other unbelieving; and so on. I know everyone will maintain that it would be commendable for a prince to have all the qualities I have just mentioned that are held to be good. But because a prince cannot wholly have or espouse all these qualities, as the human condition will not allow it, he must be wise enough to know how to evade the infamy of the qualities that are thought to be bad, which will cause him to lose his state. If possible he should also avoid the qualities which are considered bad but will not actually lose him his state, but if he must indulge in them, he need not concern himself about their consequences. He also should not concern himself about incurring the infamy of qualities that are considered bad if he needs them to save his state. For there are cases in which people might think a certain path is valourous, but following it would be the prince's ruin, while there are also cases in which a certain way might seem evil, but following it will result in the prince's safety and well-being.

CHAPTER SIXTEEN

Of generosity and parsimony

To begin with the first of these qualities: I propose that it is good to be thought generous. And yet generosity pursued in a way that makes people perceive you as generous will harm you, because if you exercise generosity in all modesty, as is appropriate, it will not be recognized, and you will not be able to avoid the reputation of miserliness. Hence, if one wishes to be perceived as generous among men, one will have to indulge in a great deal of sumptuous display. A prince who chooses this path will consume all his resources and eventually will have to overburden the populace with taxes, extort money from them, and do whatever else is necessary to raise money to maintain his reputation for being generous. This will make him hateful to his subjects, and, should he become poor, despised by all. With his generosity he will have hurt many and rewarded few. He will be vulnerable to the slightest unrest and fall prey to the first danger. When the prince who has chosen this path realizes this, his impulse is to draw back, which quickly brings him a reputation for miserliness.

Therefore a wise prince, seeing that he is unable to practise ostentatious generosity without harming himself, must not mind acquiring a reputation for miserliness. With time he will come to be considered generous once people see that his parsimony has produced sufficient funds and enabled him to defend himself from those who make war on him, and to launch campaigns without burdening the populace. In this way he will be considered generous by the great number of men from whom he takes nothing, and miserly by the few to whom he gives nothing. In our times we have seen great deeds accomplished only by those who were considered miserly; all the others came to ruin. Pope Julius II, though he made use of his reputation for generosity to gain the papacy, did not strive to maintain it afterwards. This was so that he could wage wars. The present king of France[61] has launched many wars without imposing extra taxes on his people, which he has been able to do only because the additional expenditures have been provided for by his long parsimony. The present king of Spain,[62] had he been considered generous, could not have undertaken or won so many campaigns. Consequently, a prince must care little about gaining a reputation for parsimony if he does not want to rob his subjects and yet wishes to be able to defend himself without becoming poor and contemptible or being forced to become rapacious. Parsimony is one of the vices that permit him to reign.

Were someone to argue that Caesar acquired his empire through generosity, and that many others achieved the highest ranks because they were generous and were seen as such, my answer is: Either you are already a prince, or you are on your way to becoming one. In the first case, such generosity is damaging; in the second, it is quite necessary to be considered generous. Caesar was one of those who wanted to rule Rome. However, had he survived after he gained his principality and not tempered his spending, he would have destroyed Rome. But were someone to counter that there have been many princes who were considered most generous and who did great things with their armies, I would reply: A prince spends either his own wealth, or that of his subjects or of others. In the first case he must be frugal, while in the second, he must show every generosity. A prince who rides out with his army, sustaining himself by looting, sacking, and plundering, controlling the assets of others, such a prince needs to be generous. Otherwise his soldiers will not follow him. And it is easier to be a generous giver when the possessions you are giving away are not your own or those of your subjects. Cyrus, Caesar, and Alexander were of this class. Spending what belongs to others does not diminish your standing but

---

61. Louis XII.
62. Ferdinand II.

increases it. Only spending what is your own harms you. There is nothing that consumes itself like generosity: The more you use it, the more you lose the capacity of using it. You either become poor and disdained, or, to escape poverty, rapacious and hated. There is nothing a prince must avoid more than being at once disdained and hated, and generosity leads to both. It is therefore wiser to settle for a reputation of miserliness which incurs disdain without hatred, than to try to gain a reputation for generosity that brings with it a reputation for rapacity, incurring disdain with hatred.

CHAPTER SEVENTEEN

OF CRUELTY AND MERCY,
AND WHETHER IT IS BETTER
TO BE LOVED THAN FEARED,
OR THE CONTRARY

Proceeding to the other qualities I have already mentioned,[63] I maintain that every prince must wish to be considered merciful and not cruel. Nevertheless, he must avoid using mercy inappropriately. Cesare Borgia was considered cruel, yet his cruelty brought order to the Romagna, uniting it and making it peaceful and loyal. All things considered, Borgia proved far more merciful than the people of Florence, who allowed Pistoia to be destroyed simply in order to avoid a reputation for cruelty. A prince, therefore, must not fear being reproached for cruelty when it is a matter of keeping his subjects united and loyal, because with a few exemplary executions he will be more merciful than those who, through too much mercy, allow the kind of disorder to spread that gives rise to plunder and murder. This harms the whole community, while an execution ordered by a prince harms only a single individual.

Unlike an established prince, a new prince cannot escape a reputation for cruelty, since newly acquired states are filled with danger. As Virgil has Dido say: *Res dura, et regni novitas me talia cogunt / Moliri, et late fines custode tueri* (The harsh situation and the newness of my kingdom force me to act this way and post guards at my borders).

63. Chapter 15, paragraph 2.

Nevertheless, a prince must not be quick to believe the worst and act impulsively, becoming afraid of his own shadow. His actions must be tempered by prudence and humanity so that too much trust does not render him incautious, nor too much mistrust intolerable.

This raises the question whether it is better to be loved than feared, or the contrary. My reply is that one would like to be both, but as it is difficult to combine love and fear, if one has to choose between them it is far safer to be feared than loved. Because it can be said of men that they are ungrateful and inconstant, simulators and dissimulators,[64] and that they are hungry for profit and quick to evade danger. While you do them good they are devoted to you, offering you their lives, their possessions, their children, as I have said before – but only as long as danger is far off. The moment danger is at hand, they turn away. A prince who has based everything on their word without taking other precautions is ruined, because friendships acquired at a price and not through magnanimity and nobility of spirit can be bought but not owned, nor do they bring a return in difficult times. Men have less compunction about harming someone who has made himself loved than harming someone who has made himself feared, because love is held in place by chains of obligation, which, as men are evil, will quickly be broken if self-interest is at stake. But fear is held in place by a dread of punishment, which one can always rely on.

The prince, however, must make himself feared so that he avoids hatred, even if he does not acquire love. Being feared and not hated go well together, and the prince can always achieve this if he does not touch the property or the women of his citizens and subjects. If he finds he must execute someone, he should do so only if there is adequate justification and a manifest cause. But above all he must refrain from seizing the property of others, because a man is quicker to forget the death of his father than the loss of his patrimony. Furthermore, there are always ample reasons for seizing another's property, and he who begins to live by plunder will always find reasons to take what be-

---

64. Sallust, in his account of the Catiline conspiracy in *De conjuratione Catilinae*, described Catiline as *simulator ac dissimulator*.

longs to others, whereas the reasons for having to execute someone are rare, and frequently altogether lacking.[65]

Yet when a prince is with his army and has a multitude of soldiers under his command, he must not scruple about gaining a reputation for cruelty, because without it he can never keep his army united or willing to follow him into battle. One of Hannibal's many admirable achievements was that he marched his enormous army of myriad nationalities into battle in foreign lands. Whether Fortune smiled on him or not, there was never any dissension among them nor any rebellion against him. The only reason for this was his inhumane cruelty, which, combined with his infinite skill, made him venerated and feared in the eyes of his men. Without this quality, his other abilities would not have produced this effect. Some careless historians admire this quality while condemning the principal reason for it.

That his other abilities would not have sufficed to keep his army in check can be seen from the example of Scipio, an exceptional man not only in his time, but in all of history. His army rebelled in Spain for no other reason than his undue lenience, which allowed the soldiers more freedom than is suitable in military discipline. He was reproached for this in the Senate by Fabius Maximus, who called him the corrupter of the Roman army. The Locrians had been savaged and plundered by one of Scipio's officers, after which Scipio neither made reparations nor punished the officer, a consequence of Scipio's easygoing nature.[66] Subsequently, a Locrian spoke before the Senate and, in an attempt to excuse Scipio, said that there were many men who were better at not transgressing than they were at punishing the transgressions of others. With time, Scipio's nature would have thrown a shadow on his fame

65. Machiavelli develops these ideas in *Discourses*, Book III, chapter 6: 'The injury princes do to citizens is usually against their property, their honour, or their life. In the case of injury against life, threats are more dangerous than executions. In fact, threats are extremely dangerous, while executions are not at all: He who is dead cannot think about revenge, while he who remains alive will usually leave such thoughts to the dead.'

66. Livy (Book XXIX, chapter 8) writes: 'But Pleminius so surpassed General Hamilcar in crime and greed – the Roman soldiers so surpassing the Carthaginians – that they seemed to be rivalling one another not in battle but in vice. Nothing that renders the power of the strong hateful to the weak was left undone by the Roman general and his soldiers toward the townspeople.'

and glory had he been a general in the times of the empire, but as he lived under the government of the Senate, this weakness was not only concealed, but brought him glory.

Returning to the question of being feared or loved, I conclude that since men love at their own will and fear at the will of the prince, a wise prince must build a foundation on what is his own, and not on what belongs to others. At the same time, he must do all in his power to escape being hated, as I have already said.

CHAPTER EIGHTEEN

OF THE NEED FOR PRINCES
TO KEEP THEIR WORD

Everyone knows how commendable it is for a prince to keep his word and live by integrity rather than by cunning. And yet our own era has shown that princes who have little regard for their word have achieved great things, being expert at beguiling men's minds. In the end, these princes overcame those who relied solely on loyalty.

There are two ways of fighting: either with laws or with force. The first is peculiar to men, the second to beasts. But because the first way often does not suffice, one has to resort to the second. Nevertheless, a prince must be expert in using both. This has been taught to princes allegorically by ancient writers, who tell us that Achilles and many other ancient princes were sent to Chiron the Centaur to be raised and tutored. What this means is that the ancient princes, whose tutor was half man and half beast, learned to use both natures, neither of which can prevail without the other.

Since a prince must know how to use the nature of the beast to his advantage, he must emulate both the fox and the lion, because a lion cannot defy a snare, while a fox cannot defy a pack of wolves. A prince must therefore be a fox to spot the snares, and a lion to overwhelm the wolves. The prince who models himself only on the lion does not grasp this, but a wise ruler cannot and should not keep his word when it would be to his disadvantage to do so, and when the reasons that made him give his word have disappeared. If all men were good, this rule would not stand. But as men are wicked and not prepared to keep their word to you, you have no need to keep your word to them. Nor does a prince ever lack legitimate pretexts for concealing the fact that he has broken his word. There are countless examples from our times of the many peace treaties and promises that have been rendered null and void through the fickleness of princes. The princes who have best used the nature of the fox to their advantage have been the most successful. But one must know how to conceal this quality and be a great simulator and dissimulator,[67] for men are so simple, and so prone to being won over by the necessity of the moment, that a deceiver will always find someone willing to be deceived.

There is an example from recent times that I do not want to pass over. Pope Alexander VI never thought or did anything except to deceive, and he always found someone to deceive. Never has a man made more grandiose promises or sworn greater oaths, and kept them less. And yet he always got away with his deceptions, because he was so well acquainted with this aspect of the world.

Consequently, although a prince need not have all the good qualities that I have mentioned, it is most necessary for him to appear to have them.[68] I will even be so bold as to say that it actually does a prince harm to have those good qualities and always observe them. But appearing to have them will benefit him. Of course, it is best to both seem and be merciful, loyal, humane, upright, and scrupulous. And yet one's spirit should be calculated in such a way that one can, if need be, turn one's back on these qualities and become the opposite. It is vital to understand that a prince, particularly a new prince, cannot afford to cultivate attributes for which men are considered good. In order to maintain the state, a prince will often be compelled to work against what is merciful, loyal, humane, upright, and scrupulous. He must have a spirit that can change depending on the winds and variations of Fortune, and, as I have said above, he must not, if he is able, distance himself from what is good, but must also, when necessary, know how to prefer what is bad.

Therefore a prince must be very careful that no word escape his

---

67. See text for note 64 above.

68. This idea is also echoed in Machiavelli's *Discourses*, Book I, chapter 25: 'Men cherish something that seems like the real thing as much as they do the real thing itself. In fact, they are often more affected by that which seems than by that which is.'

mouth that is not filled with the five qualities I have mentioned. When one sees and hears him, he should be a paragon of mercy, loyalty, humaneness, integrity, and scrupulousness. Indeed, there is nothing more important than appearing to have this last quality. Men in general judge more with the eye than with the hand, because everyone can see, but few can feel. Everyone sees what you seem to be, but few feel what you are, and those few will not dare oppose the opinion of the many who have the majesty of the state behind them: In the actions of all men, and particularly the prince, where there is no higher justice to appeal to, one looks at the outcome.

The prince must acquire and keep his principality, and the means by which he does this will always be praised and judged honourable by all, because the common people will be convinced by appearances and by the end result. And the world is made up of common people, among whom the few dissenters who can see beyond appearances do not count when the majority can point to the prince's success. A certain prince of our times (whom I shall not name) preaches nothing but peace and loyalty, while he could not be more hostile to both.[69] Yet if he lived by what he preaches, he would by now have lost both his reputation and his state many times over.

---

69. Almost certainly an allusion to Ferdinand II.

CHAPTER NINETEEN

Of how to avoid contempt
and hatred

As I have already discussed the most important qualities[70] that attract praise or blame, I would like to touch on others in more general terms, so that the prince may note (as I have to some extent mentioned) how to avoid the things that would make him hated and scorned.[71] If he manages to do this he will have accomplished his duty, and will not face any risk should he perpetrate other infamies. What will make him hated above all, as I have said, is rapaciousness and seizing the property and women of his subjects, which he must refrain from. Men will generally live contentedly as long as their property and honour are not touched, and the prince need only counter the ambition of a few, which can be done easily and in many ways. What will make the prince contemptible is for him to be perceived as undependable, frivolous, effeminate, pusillanimous and irresolute, against which a prince must guard himself as from the plague. He must do his utmost so that his actions will be perceived as imbued with greatness, courage, dignity and power. And as for the private affairs of his subjects, he must be adamant that his decisions are irrevocable. He must maintain a standing such that no man would venture to cheat or deceive him.

70. See chapter 15, in which Machiavelli discusses 'the qualities that attract praise or blame.'
71. Throughout this chapter Machiavelli touches on ideas put forward in Aristotle's *Politics*, Book V. Aristotle writes (Book V, chapter 10, 1312b, 20): 'There are two principal reasons that lead men to attack tyrannies: hatred and scorn.'

A prince who creates this opinion of himself will be greatly esteemed, and it is difficult to attack or conspire against one who is greatly esteemed, so long as he is perceived as excellent and is revered by his people. But a prince must have two fears: one internal, based on his subjects; the other external, based on foreign powers. From the foreign enemy the prince can defend himself with good arms and good friends (and he who has good arms will always have good friends); and internal matters will always be stable when external matters are stable, so long as they have not been clouded by conspiracy. But even if external matters are volatile, the prince will always counter every violence if he has lived and ruled as I have mentioned and does not lose courage (as I have said Nabis of Sparta did).[72]

When external affairs are stable, the prince must still fear that his subjects might conspire secretly against him. But he will be quite safe from this as long as he avoids being hated or despised and keeps the populace on his side. It is important that he do this, as I have said at length above. One of the strongest remedies a prince has against conspiracy is not to be hated by the masses, because conspirators are invariably certain that they will satisfy the populace by killing the prince. But if on the other hand they think they will enrage the populace, they will not pluck up the courage for such an act, because the difficulties facing conspirators are infinite. Experience has taught that there have been many conspiracies, but few that have ended well, because whoever conspires cannot do so alone, nor can he attract cohorts other than those who he believes are malcontents. And the moment you take a malcontent into your confidence, you give him the opportunity to become quite content, pursuing his own advantage by betraying you.[73] So much so, that seeing the certain gain in that direction, and seeing doubt and peril in the other, it must be a rare friend or a most determined enemy of the prince who will keep his word to you.

In short, from the conspirator's point of view there is nothing but fear, rivalry, and the prospect of horrific punishment, whereas from the prince's perspective there are the majesty of the principality, the laws,

72. See chapter 9.
73. Machiavelli writes in *Discourses*, Book III, chapter 6: 'If on the other hand you measure faithfulness by the discontent an ally has for the prince, you can be quite deceived, because the instant you take this malcontent into your confidence you provide him with the opportunity to become quite content at your expense.'

and the protection afforded by friends and the state. If one also adds the goodwill of the people, it is unlikely that anyone would be so bold as to conspire against the prince, since under normal circumstances conspirators have much to fear before committing the evil deed, but in this case they have just as much to fear afterwards, as they will have the whole populace against them. Once their deed is done, they cannot hope for refuge anywhere.

I could cite infinite examples of this, but shall limit myself to one incident that took place within the memory of our fathers. Annibale Bentivoglio, the Prince of Bologna and grandfather of the present Annibale Bentivoglio, was killed by the Canneschi, who conspired against him, leaving no one to succeed him except his son Giovanni, at that time still in swaddling clothes. Immediately after the murder, the people rose and killed all the Canneschi, a result of the people's goodwill toward the house of Bentivoglio. In all Bologna, after Annibale's death, there were no heirs who could rule the state, but the people's goodwill was so great that when they heard that there was a Bentivoglio living in Florence, who had been thought to be the son of a blacksmith, they went there to offer him the government of Bologna, which he accepted until young Giovanni Bentivoglio came of age.

I therefore conclude that a prince need not worry unduly about conspiracies when the people are well disposed toward him. But if they are his enemies and hate him, he must fear everything and everybody. Well-ordered states and wise princes have been careful not to anger the nobles and to keep the populace content, because this is one of the most important tasks that falls on a prince.

Among the well-ordered and well-governed states of our times is France. It has countless good institutions on which the king's liberty and security depend, of which the foremost is the *parlement* and its authority.[74] For he who set up this system was aware of the nobles' insolence and ambition and deemed that they needed a harness to keep them in check, but he was also aware of the people's hatred of the nobles, a hatred based on fear. The idea was to assuage both factions, but

---

74. The French *parlements* formed the supreme court under the Ancien Régime in France, divided into the Parisian *parlement*, which was the most powerful, and the regional *parlements*. The *parlements* saw to it that the king's edicts and measures conformed with the principles of law and justice. They provided a counterbalance to royal power. By Machiavelli's time, the *parlements* had adopted a course of systematic opposition to the king.

without the king's being seen to be involved. This removed any allegations the nobles might make that the king was favouring the populace, or any allegations the populace might make that he was favouring the nobles. This was the reason for establishing an independent institution that could keep the nobles in check, and favour the people without compromising the king. Such a decision could not have been better or more wise, nor could there be a better guarantee for the security of the king and the kingdom. From which one can draw another notable principle: Princes must delegate difficult tasks to others and keep popular ones for themselves. Once more I conclude that a prince has to respect the nobles, but must not make himself hated by the populace.

Many who have considered the way that certain Roman emperors lived and died might argue that they present examples that contradict my opinions, as some of these emperors did live excellently, showing much skill and spirit, but nevertheless lost their throne or were killed by their own men who conspired against them. I will respond to these objections by discussing the qualities of a few emperors, demonstrating that the reasons for their ruin are in accord with what I have cited. This should be of interest to anyone reading about the events of that era. I will limit myself to the emperors who came to the throne between the reigns of Marcus the Philosopher and Maximinus. These were Marcus, his son Commodus, Pertinax, Julianus, Severus, his son Antoninus Caracalla, Macrinus, Elagabalus, Alexander, and Maximinus.

First of all I would like to point out that while in most principalities one merely has to contend with the ambitions of the great and the hostility of the populace, the Roman emperors had to face a third problem: contending with the cruelty and plundering of their soldiers. This was so difficult that it proved the ruin of many, since it is hard to satisfy both army and populace. The populace wants peace and hence a modest prince, while the army wants a prince with a military spirit who is arrogant, cruel, and rapacious, and ready to unleash these qualities on the populace so that the soldiers can double their pay and give free rein to their greed and cruelty. The result was that those emperors who by nature or education did not have the standing that could keep the army or the populace in check invariably came to grief. Most of these emperors, particularly those who came to power as new princes, knew the difficulty of balancing these two opposing factions and chose to reward the soldiers with little thought of how this would harm the populace. This was a necessary decision. A prince cannot avoid being hated by one of the two factions. Hence he must first strive not to be hated by the people, and should that not be possible, he should do his utmost to avoid the hatred of the faction that is more powerful. Therefore emperors who were new princes and especially needed strong backing preferred to side with the army rather than the populace. This proved to be to the emperor's benefit or not, depending on whether he knew how to maintain his standing with the army.

It was for these reasons that Marcus, Pertinax, and Alexander – modest men who loved justice, spurned cruelty, and were kind and humane – met tragic ends. All, that is, except for Marcus, who lived and died with honour. He had come to the imperial throne by inheritance and did not need to show gratitude to the army or the populace, and he was a man of great skill, which made him venerated by all. Throughout his life he kept the soldiers in check and the people within bounds, and was never hated or disdained. But Pertinax was made emperor despite the opposition of the soldiers, who had been used to living licentiously under Commodus and could not bear the honest way of life that Pertinax wanted to force on them. Pertinax inspired hatred, and as he was an old man, contempt as well, so he came to ruin at the very start of his reign. And here one must note that hatred can be caused through good deeds as much as through bad. As I have said before, a prince who wants to maintain his state is often forced not to be good, because when the faction that you believe you need in order to rule is corrupt – whether it is the populace, the army, or the nobles – it is to your advantage to satisfy them, in which case good deeds are your enemy. But let us come to Emperor Alexander, who was so good that among the many things he was praised for was that not a single man was put to death without trial during his fourteen-year reign. Nevertheless, he was considered effeminate and a man who let himself be governed by his mother. This brought derision upon him, and the army conspired against him and killed him.

Let us now discuss, in contrast, the qualities of Commodus, Severus, Antoninus Caracalla, and Maximinus, all of whom you will find most cruel and rapacious. To satisfy their soldiers they did not spare any violence that could be inflicted on the populace. All these emperors, with the exception of Severus, came to a bad end. Severus was so skilled that he managed to keep the army on his side even though he oppressed the populace, and so had a successful reign. His skill made him so formidable in the eyes of the army and the populace that the former remained satisfied and reverent, and the latter awe-struck and stupefied. For a new prince, Severus's actions were great and noteworthy, and so I would like briefly to demonstrate how well he used the traits of both the fox and the lion, which I have already re-ferred to as necessary for a prince to emulate. When Severus was gen-eral of the Roman army in Slavonia he was aware of the indolence of Emperor Julianus, and he persuaded his men to follow him to Rome to avenge the death of Pertinax, who had died at the hands of the Praeto-rian Guard. Under this pretext Severus marched his army against Rome without revealing that he had any aspirations to the imperial throne, and was in Italy before anyone even realized that he had set out. When he arrived in Rome, the Senate elected him emperor out of fear, and sentenced Julianus to death. Severus now faced two difficul-ties in asserting his authority over the whole empire: One was Asia, where Niger, general of the Asiatic armies, had had himself pro-claimed emperor, and the other was the West, where Albinus was as-piring to the throne.[75] Severus deemed it dangerous to declare himself an enemy to both men, and so decided to attack Niger and deceive Al-binus. He wrote to Albinus that although the Senate had elected him, Severus, emperor, he wanted to share the throne with Albinus, and was sending him the title of Caesar. He informed him that through a pro-nouncement of the Senate he had made him his co-ruler. All of this Albinus believed. But no sooner had Severus defeated and killed Niger, bringing Asia under his control, than he returned to Rome and denounced Albinus in the Senate, charging that Albinus was plotting to kill him instead of showing gratitude for the favours he had been ac-corded. Severus announced that he was compelled to punish Albinus's ingratitude. He confronted him in France and took from him his state and his life.

Whoever considers Severus's actions will see that he was a fero-cious lion and a cunning fox, feared and revered by all, and not hated

<hr />

75. General Pescennius Niger was proclaimed emperor by his legions when Emperor Com-modus's successor, Pertinax, was murdered in the spring of 193 CE, becoming ruler of the Greek-speaking East. General Albinus represented the aristocracy of the Latin-speaking West, and was an imperial candidate in the years 193-197 CE.

by the army. One should not be surprised that as a new prince he managed to secure so much authority, for his exceptional standing always shielded him from the hatred that his rapaciousness might have sparked among the people.

Severus's son Antoninus was also a man with qualities that made him formidable in the eyes of the people and popular with his soldiers.[76] He was a military man who could bear any hardship and who scorned delicate dishes and every other weakness. This raised him in the esteem of his soldiers. Nevertheless, Antoninus's ferocity and cruelty were so great and so unprecedented – after untold murders he had a large part of the population of Rome and the entire populace of Alexandria put to death – that all the world came to despise him. Antoninus was feared even by his own entourage, which resulted in his being killed by a centurion in the midst of his own army. From which it is to be noted that a prince cannot avoid assassination resulting from the deliberations of a determined mind, because he can be assaulted by anyone who does not care about dying himself. A prince need not fear this unduly, because such men are very rare.[77] He has only to refrain from inflicting grave injury on those who serve him and whom he keeps about himself in service of the state. Antoninus did inflict such injury, shamefully killing the brother of one of his own centurions and threatening the centurion every day, even though he retained him as his bodyguard.[78] Such rash conduct was bound to bring about his own ruin, and it did.

But let us come to Commodus, who, having inherited his throne from his father, Emperor Marcus, should have been able to hold on to it with ease. He had only to follow in his father's footsteps to satisfy both the army and the people, but he had a cruel and feral nature. In order to exercise his rapacity on the populace, he chose to favour the

---

76. Machiavelli follows Herodian's description in *History of the Empire*, Book IV, particularly chapters 4–9.

77. Aristotle (*Politics*, Book V, chapter 11, 1315a, 24) writes: 'Among those who plot to assassinate the tyrant, those who are most worrisome, and should be most carefully watched, are those who do not strive to preserve their own lives while destroying his.'

78. Aristotle (*Politics*, Book V, chapter 11, 1315a, 27) writes: 'Therefore the ruler must be extremely wary of those who believe that he has harmed them or those under their care.' King Agis IV (d. 241 BCE) attempted to introduce sweeping reforms that drew on Sparta's legendary lawgiver Lycurgus (c. seventh century BCE). Agis was, however, assassinated in the fourth year of his reign.

army, and allowed it every dissipation. Furthermore, he did not maintain his dignity, often descending into the arenas to fight with gladiators and doing other things that were contemptible and unworthy of imperial majesty, becoming a figure of scorn in the eyes of the soldiers. Being hated on one hand and scorned on the other, he was conspired against and killed.

It remains for us to consider the qualities of Maximinus. He was extremely pugnacious, but as the army had become weary of Alexander's weakness, which I discussed above, when he died, they elected Maximinus to the imperial throne. But Maximinus did not rule for long. Two things made him hated and disdained: First, he came from a very humble background, having herded sheep in Thrace (a fact that was widely known and looked down upon by all), and second, at the beginning of his reign he resisted going to Rome to take possession of the imperial throne. He also gave the impression of being unusually cruel, since through his prefects he had exercised great brutality in Rome and throughout the empire. As a result, everyone was filled with contempt for his lowly birth and with hatred that arose from fear of his ferocity. First Africa rebelled, then the Senate and the populace of Rome, and finally all of Italy conspired against him. His own soldiers rebelled during a difficult siege of Aquileia, and, tired of his cruelty and fearing him less because he had so many enemies, they killed him.

I will not discuss Elagabalus, Macrinus, or Julianus, who were so widely disdained that they were quickly eliminated, but shall come to the conclusion of this discourse. The princes of our era do not face the Roman emperors' problem of having to indulge their soldiers by unlawful means, though they do have to make some concessions to them. Issues are now resolved quickly, as none of our princes have the kind of established armies that evolved with the government and with the administration of the provinces, as was the case in imperial Rome. If in Roman times it was necessary to favour the army more than the people, that was because the soldiers carried more weight than the people. Now it is necessary for all princes, except the Ottoman sultan and the Sultan of Egypt, to favour the people above the army, because it is the people who carry more weight. But I make an exception of the Ottoman sultan: He always surrounds himself with an infantry of twelve thousand and a cavalry of fifteen thousand, on which the security and power of his rule depend. For him it is vital that he set aside all other considerations and keep his soldiers well disposed. Similarly, the Egyptian sultan's rule is also entirely in the hands of his soldiers, and so it behoves him to keep them on his side without consideration for the populace. It should be noted that the principality of the Egyptian sultan differs from other principalities in that it is similar to the Christian pontificate, which cannot be called a hereditary principality or a new principality because it is not the sons of the old prince who are the heirs and rulers. Princes are elected to that rank by those who have the authority to do so. As the Egyptian sultanate is an old institution, one cannot call it a new principality because it does not bring with it any of the difficulties of new principalities. Even if the prince is new, the institutions of that state are old and set up to receive him as if he were a hereditary ruler.

But let us return to our subject. If one weighs the above discourse, it is clear that it was hatred or contempt that brought about the ruin of the emperors I have mentioned. Though some followed one path and some the other, in each case some of the emperors ended well and some badly. It was futile and disastrous for Pertinax and Alexander, as new princes, to imitate Marcus, who was a hereditary ruler, and it was just as disastrous for Caracalla, Commodus, and Maximinus to imitate Severus, as they did not have the skill to follow in his footsteps. A new prince in a new principality cannot imitate the exploits of Marcus, but neither should he imitate those of Severus. He must take from Severus the necessary attributes to found a new state, and from Marcus the glorious attributes suitable for conserving a state that is already established and stable.

CHAPTER TWENTY

OF WHETHER FORTRESSES AND MANY OTHER THINGS PRINCES CREATE EVERY DAY ARE USEFUL

In order to hold their states securely, some princes disarm their subjects, others keep their conquered territories divided, while still others encourage hostility against themselves. Still others turn to winning over those whom they suspected at the beginning of their rule. Some princes build fortresses, others destroy them. Even though one cannot lay down a definite rule concerning these choices unless one examines the particulars of the states in question, I will nevertheless discuss this in as broad terms as the topic will allow.

No new prince has ever disarmed his subjects. In fact, whenever a prince found his new subjects disarmed, he has always armed them, because when he does so those arms become his. The men he did not trust become faithful, those who were faithful remain so, and his subjects become his partisans. And yet the prince cannot arm all his subjects, so when the ones he does arm receive benefits, he need not worry unduly about the rest: The armed subjects see that they are being preferred and are bound to the prince, while the others excuse the prince for showing preference, judging it necessary that those bearing arms should receive greater rewards since they have to shoulder more duties and face greater danger. But when you start to disarm them, they take offence. You show that you mistrust them, either out of cowardice or because you have little faith in them, both of which opinions will generate hatred toward you. Because you cannot remain unarmed, you will then have to turn to a mercenary army, which is of the quality that I have already described.[79] Even if the mercenary army is good, it can never be good enough to defend you from powerful enemies and subjects you cannot trust. But as I have already said, new princes in new principalities have always armed their subjects. History is filled with such examples. Only when a prince acquires a new state added like a limb to his old state[80] is it necessary for him to disarm the new state, unless his new subjects are his partisans, but even they, over time, must be made soft and effeminate, and things must be organized so that all the arms in the prince's state are in the hands of his actual soldiers who have been at his side in his old state.

Our forefathers, and those we thought wise, used to say that Pistoia was to be held by factions and Pisa by fortresses.[81] They therefore encouraged conflicts in some of their subject cities so they could hold them more easily. In those days, when there was a certain equilibrium in Italy, this might have been a good strategy, but I do not see how one can live by this principle today, because I do not believe that such divisions ever do anyone any good. In fact, it is inevitable that a divided city will fall the instant an enemy attacks: The weaker faction will ally itself with the external force, while the stronger faction will not be able to hold out.

I believe that the Venetians incited the Guelph and Ghibelline factions in the cities under their control for the reasons I have just mentioned.[82] The Venetians never actually let them shed each other's blood, but they did encourage their differences, so that the Guelphs and Ghibellines, occupied as they were with each other, did not unite against the Venetians. Yet as we have subsequently seen, this did not turn out to Venice's advantage, because when she was defeated at Vailà, one of the factions was quick to take courage and seize the whole state from her.[83] This strategy indicates weakness in a prince, because in a strong principality such divisions are never permitted. They bring advantages only in times of peace, enabling the prince to manage his sub-

79. See chapter 12.
80. See chapter 3.
81. See chapter 17.
82. The Guelphs supported the papacy and the Ghibellines the Holy Roman Emperors.
83. The Venetians were defeated in 1509 in the Battle of Agnadello by the forces of the League of Cambrai, after which the Ghibelline faction gained the upper hand in Venice.

jects with greater ease. But when war comes, this strategy reveals its flaws.

Without doubt, princes become great when they overcome difficulties and hurdles put in their path. When Fortune wants to advance a new prince, for whom it is more vital to acquire prestige than it is for a hereditary prince, she creates enemies for him, making them launch campaigns against him so that he is compelled to overcome them and climb higher on the ladder that they have brought him. Therefore, many judge that a wise prince must skilfully fan some enmity whenever the opportunity arises, so that in crushing it he will increase his standing.

Princes, particularly new ones, have found more loyalty and value in the men they distrusted at the beginning of their reign than in those who were considered sound. Pandolfo Petrucci, the Prince of Siena, ruled his state relying more on men he had initially distrusted than on his first supporters. But one cannot lay this matter out in broad terms, since it varies with every case. I will only say that men who are enemies of the prince at the beginning of his reign, but who are of quality and who need his support to maintain their position, can be won over with great ease. These men will be forced to serve him the more loyally, as they are aware that it is vital to rescind the negative opinion the prince initially had of them. Hence they are of greater use to him than are men who serve him with too much confidence in his goodwill and thus neglect his affairs.

Since our topic requires it, I do not wish to omit reminding princes who have recently acquired a state with the help of a faction within it that they should weigh the reasons that might have moved this faction to support them. If it is not natural affection toward the prince that made it favour him, but rather discontent with the former government, it will be only with much toil and difficulty that the prince will maintain these malcontents as his allies, because it will be impossible to satisfy them. If he looks closely at what can be deduced from ancient and modern examples, he will see that it is far easier to win over men who were content with the state before he conquered it, and therefore were his enemies, than to win over those who had not been satisfied, and so became his allies and supported his occupation of the state.

In order that princes might hold their states more securely, it has been their custom to build fortresses to act as a check on those who might have designs against them and to have a secure refuge against sudden rebellion. I praise this, as it has been a long-standing practice. And yet in our own times Niccolò Vitelli tore down two fortresses in Città di Castello in order to hold on to that state, while Guido Ubaldo, the Duke of Urbino, when he returned to his dominions from which Cesare Borgia had driven him, razed all the fortresses of that province to the ground, judging that he would be less likely to lose his state a second time without them. The Bentivogli, returning to Bologna, employed similar measures. Therefore, fortresses can be useful or not, depending on the times. If they are useful in one way, they can harm you in another. The question can be considered in this light: The prince who fears his people more than he does a foreign enemy must build fortresses, but the prince who fears a foreign enemy more than he does his people should not. The Castle of Milan built by Francesco Sforza has done and will do more harm to the House of Sforza than any turmoil in that state. The best fortress for the prince is to be loved by his people, because if he is hated by them, all the fortresses in the world will not save him. Once the populace has taken up arms, there will always be a foreign power eager to come to its aid.

In our time, we have not seen fortresses to be of any use to princes, except in the case of the Countess of Forlì when her husband, Count Girolamo, was killed. She managed to escape her people's uprising by retiring to her fortress and waiting there to recover her state with the help of Milan:[84] At that point in history, circumstances were such that a foreign power could not come to the aid of the people. But later the countess's fortresses were of little help to her when a foreign power – Cesare Borgia – attacked, and the populace, hostile to her, joined forces with him. Both then and before, it would have been safer for the countess to be loved by her people than to have fortresses. All things considered, I will praise both the prince who builds fortresses and the prince who does not, but I shall blame the prince who relies on his fortresses and thinks nothing of being hated by the people.

---

84. Caterina Sforza Riario (1463–1509) was the ruler of Imola and Forlì. When her husband, Girolamo Riario, was assassinated in 1488, she held out against the rebels in one of her fortresses until help arrived from her uncle, Ludovico Sforza of Milan. (Negotiations with Caterina Sforza Riario were the subject of Machiavelli's very first diplomatic assignment in July 1499.)

CHAPTER TWENTY-ONE

OF WHAT A PRINCE SHOULD DO

TO ACQUIRE PRESTIGE

Nothing can bring a prince more esteem than great feats and extraordinary actions. In our time we have Ferdinand of Aragon, the present king of Spain, who could almost be called a new prince because he started out as a weak monarch, but through fame and glory has become the foremost king of Christendom. If you consider his deeds, you will find that they are great, some of them even extraordinary. At the beginning of his reign he attacked Granada, an exploit that was to establish the cornerstone of his state. He did this quite casually, without the least concern that anyone might hinder him. He kept the attention of the barons of Castile trained on his enterprise, and, with their minds on this war, they did not think of introducing any changes. Before they realized what was happening, he had overshadowed them in prestige and power. He managed to build up his army with funds from the Church and the people, and during the long war in Granada he firmly established this army, which subsequently brought him much honour. To launch ever greater campaigns, he invariably made use of religion, resorting to a pious cruelty, robbing the Marranos[85] and routing them from his kingdom. No example of an extraordinary act is more pitiful and strange. Under the same mantle he attacked Africa. He campaigned in Italy, recently invaded France, and has always plotted and

85. Spanish Jews who converted to Christianity but continued practising Judaism secretly.

carried out great feats that have captured the imagination of his people and kept their eyes on the outcome. He has launched these exploits in such quick succession that he has never given anyone an opportunity to conspire against him.

It also befits a prince to take extraordinary action in internal affairs, such as the exploits told of Bernabò of Milan.[86] When someone does something in civil life that is extraordinarily good or bad, the prince should find a way to reward or punish this person that will be much talked about. Above all, a prince must endeavour in all his actions to give the impression of being a superior man of extraordinary intelligence.

A prince is also revered when he is a true friend and a true enemy – in other words, when he declares himself without reservation in favour of one man against another. This kind of resolution is always more useful than if he remains neutral, because if two powerful neighbours come to blows, these neighbours will either be of the kind where you have to fear the winner, or not. In either case it will be more useful for you to take a position and wage an honest war. In the case where you have to fear the winner, if you do not commit yourself, you will fall prey to whoever wins, to the delight and satisfaction of whoever loses. Neither side will have reason or cause to come to your assistance, for the winner will not want the kind of ally who did not come to his aid in adversity, nor will the loser give you refuge, since you were not prepared to share his fate with your weapons drawn.

Antiochus was summoned to Greece by the Aetolians to expel the Romans. He sent orators to the Achaeans, who were allies of Rome, urging them to remain neutral, while Roman orators were urging them to take up arms for the Roman cause. The Achaeans weighed the matter in their council. When Antiochus's emissary argued that they should stay neutral, the Roman emissary replied: 'Though they tell you not to intervene in our war, nothing would be further from your interests. Once you have lost esteem and character, you will end up as the victor's prize' (*Quod autem isti dicunt non interponendi vos bello, nihil*

---

86. Bernabò Visconti (1323–85), Lord of Milan, raised spectacular sums of money by unscrupulous taxation to fight constant wars, and gained great influence throughout Europe by providing enormous dowries for his many illegitimate daughters, whom he married off strategically to the European, particularly German, high nobility. (Among his sons-in-law were Leopold III of Austria, Stephan III of Bavaria, and Eberhard III of Württemberg.)

magis alienum rebus vestris est; sine gratia, sine dignitate, praemium victoris eritis).[87] He who is not your ally will always urge you to remain neutral, while your ally will urge you to come to his aid with your arms. The irresolute prince will most often follow the path of neutrality in order to avoid immediate danger, and will most often come to ruin. But when a prince boldly declares himself for one of the two sides, even if that side wins and is powerful and he remains in principle at its mercy, that side will be obliged to him and bound by contract of allegiance, and men are never so deceitful that they would subjugate someone in such a striking display of ingratitude after he had come to their aid. Furthermore, victories are never so decisive that the victor can wholly disregard justice. If the prince supported the losing side, that side will receive him and help him to the extent that it can, and he will become its companion in a destiny that may well resurge once more.

When they who fight one another are such that you need not fear whoever wins, it is all the more prudent for you to take sides. That way, you instigate the ruin of a ruler with the help of another ruler, who, were he wise, would be eager to save him. In this case, it is impossible for the side you are helping not to win, and in winning it remains in your debt. Here I would like to note that a prince should avoid forming an alliance with a power stronger than himself merely in order to attack another, unless, as I have said before, necessity compels him. Because if that power wins, he will end up its prisoner, and princes must do their utmost to avoid ending up in another's power. The Venetians allied themselves with France against the Duke of Milan even though they could have avoided this alliance, and it resulted in their ruin. If one cannot avoid such an alliance, as happened with the Florentines when the armies of the pope and Spain attacked Lombardy, then the prince must enter alliances for the reasons I have given. Nor should any state believe it can always make secure choices: In fact, all choices should be considered dubious, because it is in the nature of things that you can never escape one setback without running into another. Wisdom consists of knowing how to recognize the respective qualities of the setbacks and choosing the lesser evil.[88]

A prince must also prove himself someone who admires ability, fur-

87. A slightly altered quotation from Livy, Book XXXV, chapter 49.
88. Machiavelli writes in *Discourses*, Book I, chapter 6: 'If one looks carefully, this pattern can be observed in all human affairs: One can never remove one problem without another one's arising.'

thering skilful men and honouring those who excel in what they do. He must also make certain that his citizens can go about their work unhampered – in trade, agriculture, and all the other professions – so that no one will be afraid of accumulating possessions out of fear that they might be taken away, or afraid of starting a business for fear of taxes. The prince must reward whoever wants to do these things and whoever wants to improve either the city or the state in some way. Furthermore, at certain times of the year, he has to keep the population busy with feasts and spectacles, and, as every city is divided into guilds and clans, he must also keep those groups in mind, meeting with them from time to time, and always showing himself as humane and munificent. He must always remain within the bounds of his majesty and dignity, which must never be absent.

CHAPTER TWENTY-TWO

OF THE ADVISERS OF PRINCES

The choice of advisers is very important for a prince: Advisers are able or not, depending on the prince's wisdom. One can assess a prince's intelligence by looking at the men with whom he surrounds himself. If they are capable and loyal, one can consider the prince prudent, because he was able to discern their ability and managed to keep them loyal. But when these men are lacking in quality, one can consider the prince as deficient, because it is in choosing his advisers that he can make his first mistake. Anyone who knew Antonio da Venafro, the minister of Pandolfo Petrucci, Prince of Siena, considered Pandolfo a most capable man for having chosen da Venafro.

There are three kinds of intelligence: One kind can understand on its own, the second can understand through others, and the third can understand neither on its own nor through others. The first kind is excellent, the second good enough, the third useless. Hence, if Pandolfo was not in the first category, he was at least in the second, because even if a prince does not possess great intelligence, if he can judge the good or bad that a man says or does, then he can distinguish between his adviser's good and bad deeds, and praise the good and punish the bad. The adviser cannot hope to deceive him, and so behaves well.

There is a dependable method by which a prince can know his adviser. When the prince sees that the adviser is more intent on furthering his own interest than that of the prince, and that his actions aim to further his own goals, this adviser will never be a good one, and the prince will never be able to trust him. A man who has the prince's affairs of state in hand must never think of himself but always of the prince, and must never involve the prince in matters that have nothing to do with him. And yet the prince, in order to keep the adviser loyal, must not forget to honour him and make him rich, obliging him by sharing with him honours and responsibilities, so that the adviser sees that he cannot exist without the prince. But the prince must also ensure that these many honours do not lead the adviser to desire even more honours, nor that great wealth lead him to desire even greater wealth, nor that his many responsibilities make him fear change. If advisers and princes are of this kind, they can have confidence in one another. If they are not, then things will end badly for one or the other.

CHAPTER TWENTY-THREE

OF THE WAY IN WHICH FLATTERERS
MUST BE AVOIDED

I do not wish to pass over an important point, a danger that a prince can escape only if he is extremely careful or has chosen his advisers well. This danger is the flatterers that fill all princely courts, because men are so self-congratulatory in the things they do, and so willing to deceive themselves, that they find it difficult to escape this plague, and in attempting to escape it they often run the risk of losing their standing. The only way for a prince to guard himself from flattering adulation is to make it understood that he will not be offended if he is told the truth. Then again, however, if every man is free to tell him the truth at will, the prince quickly becomes a figure of contempt. Therefore a prudent prince must approach the matter in an altogether different way: for his government, he must choose men who are wise and give them, and nobody else, free rein to speak their minds – but only on matters on which he consults them. Nevertheless, he must confer with them on every important issue, listen to their opinions, and then reach a decision on his own and in his own way. He must give his counsellors to understand that the more freely they speak, the more he will rely on them. The prince must not listen to anyone other than these counselors, and he must carry out his decisions, unyielding in what he has decided. A prince who acts otherwise will either come to ruin because of his flatterers, or grow increasingly irresolute by following conflicting advice, which will result in his losing respect.

I would like to cite an example from our time. Father Luca, the counsellor to the current emperor Maximilian, has said of His Majesty the Emperor that he never consults anybody, yet still has never managed to do what he wants. This resulted from his behavior, which is contrary to what I advised above. The emperor is a secretive man and does not inform anyone of his plans, nor does he take advice. But when his plans become clear as he starts putting them into effect, the men surrounding him begin to caution him. As the emperor is easily swayed, he yields, abandoning his plans. Consequently, what he does one day he undoes the next. One can never tell what he wants or intends to do, nor can one rely on his decisions.

Therefore a prince must be prepared to take counsel, but only when he seeks counsel. In fact, he should discourage anyone from offering counsel when he has not asked for it. But he must be an expert questioner and a patient listener to the truth in all matters on which he does seek counsel. If the prince realizes that someone is not telling him the truth, he must show his anger.

It is a common error to consider a prince prudent not because of his nature but on account of the good counsellors with whom he surrounds himself. Yet it is an infallible rule that a prince who is not wise cannot be advised well, unless Fortune has placed him in the hands of one who is very wise and guides him in every matter. In this case the prince might fare well, but not for long, because soon enough that counsellor will seize his state from him. Yet if a prince who is lacking in wisdom takes counsel from more than one man, he will invariably be given conflicting advice and find himself unable to reconcile it on his own. The counsellors will have their own interests at heart, and the prince will not be able to keep them in check or see through their ruses. And all counsellors are of this kind, because men never turn out to be faithful unless necessity makes them. Therefore it is to be concluded that good counsel, from whomever it comes, must be sparked by the wisdom of the prince, and not that the wisdom of the prince be sparked by good counsel.

CHAPTER TWENTY-FOUR

OF REASONS WHY ITALIAN PRINCES
HAVE LOST THEIR STATES

If the strategies I have mentioned above are carefully followed, a new prince will seem like an old, established prince. He will be more stable and secure in his state than if he had developed within it, because the actions of a new prince are more closely observed than those of a hereditary prince. If these actions are seen to be skilful, they will sooner attract and bind men to the new prince than an old bloodline would, because men are more inspired by things of the present than things of the past. If men see good in the present, they are content and do not yearn for anything else. In effect, they will stand by this prince in every way, as long as he is not otherwise lacking. He will have twice the glory, having established a new principality and having strengthened it with good laws, arms, allies, and good examples, just as a prince who is born a prince will have twice the shame if he loses his principality through lack of prudence.

If one considers the rulers of our time in Italy who have lost their states – such as the King of Naples, the Duke of Milan, and others – one can discern a common military weakness, as I have already discussed at length. One will also observe that some of these rulers had the populace against them, and that others had the populace on their side but did not know how to protect themselves against the nobles. States that are powerful enough to send an army into battle can be lost only through such defects.

Philip of Macedon (not Alexander the Great's father, but the king who was defeated by Titus Quintus)[89] did not have much power compared to the might of the Romans and Greeks who were attacking him. And yet, being a military man who knew how to inspire the populace and secure himself against his nobles, he managed to sustain a war against the Greeks and Romans for many years, and though he finally had to give up a few cities, he nevertheless kept his kingdom.

Therefore our Italian princes who were established in their principalities for many years and then lost them should blame their indolence and not Fortune. In times of peace they did not think that things might change (it is a common fault not to anticipate storms when the sea is calm), and with the advent of adversity our princes thought of escape, not defence. They hoped that the populace, angered by the victors' offensive ways, would call them back. Such a strategy might be good when others are lacking, but it is a mistake to prefer this remedy over others, because you should never let yourself fall in the hope that someone will be there to help you up. Either you will not be helped up, or, if you are, your continuing safety will be in question, because your defence was not sparked by you but by your cowardice, and defences are secure and lasting only if they are sparked by your skill.

89. Philip V of Macedon (d. 179 BCE).

CHAPTER TWENTY-FIVE

ON THE EXTENT TO WHICH FORTUNE WIELDS POWER IN THE AFFAIRS OF MEN, AND ON HOW THIS IS TO BE RESISTED

I am not unaware that many believe that the things of this world are governed to such an extent by Fortune and God that men, with all their foresight, cannot change them; that in fact there is no improving them. Those who believe this deem that they need not toil and sweat, but can let themselves be governed by Fortune. This opinion has been more prevalent in our time because of the great upheavals that we have witnessed and witness every day, and which are beyond anything we could have foreseen, and there have been times when even I have to some extent inclined to this opinion. Nevertheless, Fortune seems to be the arbiter of half our actions, but she does leave us the other half, or almost the other half, in order that our free will may prevail. I would compare Fortune to one of those violent torrents that flood the plains, destroying trees and buildings, hurling earth from one place to another. Everyone flees this torrent, everyone yields to its force without being able to stand up to it. As this is the torrent's nature, man should not neglect to prepare himself with dykes and dams in times of calm, so that when the torrent rises it will gush into a channel, its force neither so harmful nor so unbridled. The same is true with Fortune, who unleashes her force in places where man has not taken skilful precautions to resist her, and so channels her force to where she knows there are no dykes or dams to hold her back. If you consider Italy, which has been the scene of so many changes and has set so many changes in motion, you will find that it is a field without dykes or dams. Had Italy been protected with the appropriate skill, as Germany, Spain, and France were, this flood either would not have caused the great changes it did or would not have come at all.

So much for opposing Fortune in general terms. To limit myself more to particulars, I would like to remark that one can see a prince prospering one day and coming to ruin the next without having changed his nature or conduct in any way. I believe this is due, first and foremost, to the causes that I have already discussed at some length, namely, that the prince who relies entirely on Fortune will fall when Fortune changes. In my view, he who conforms his course of action to the quality of the times will fare well, and conversely he whose course of action clashes with the times will fare badly. One sees that men will proceed in different ways as they strive toward the common goal of wealth and glory: Some will proceed cautiously, others recklessly; some with force, others with guile; some with patience, others rashly. And in each of these ways one can prevail. If we take two cautious men, one might attain his goal and the other not; similarly, two men might succeed through entirely different courses of action, one through caution, the other through recklessness. The reason for this is the nature of the times that either conforms to or conflicts with their courses of action. Hence two men operating differently can obtain the same result, while when two men operate in the same way, one might achieve his goal, the other not. This also depends on the turning of Fortune's wheel from good to bad, because if a man acts with caution and patience and the wheel turns in a way that favours his course of action, he will flourish; but should the wheel turn again, he will be ruined if he does not change his manner of proceeding. One cannot find a man prudent enough to be capable of adapting to these changes, because man cannot deviate from that to which nature inclines him. Moreover, if he has always prospered by walking down a certain path, it will be difficult to persuade him to leave it. Consequently, when the time comes for a cautious man to act impetuously, he will not be able to do so, and will come to ruin. Even if he could adapt his nature to the times and circumstances, his Fortune would not change.

Pope Julius II acted impetuously in everything he undertook, and he found both the times and the circumstances in such agreement with this course of action that he always succeeded. Consider the first campaign that he launched against Bologna in the days when Giovanni Bentivoglio was still alive.[90] The Venetians were not pleased, nor was the King of Spain, and as for France, Julius was still in the midst of negotiations with them over this campaign. And yet Julius, wild and impetuous as he was, set out right away, heading the campaign himself. This move stopped the Venetians and Spaniards in their tracks: the former out of fear, the latter because of their desire to regain the entire Kingdom of Naples, while the King of France found himself drawn in despite himself. Seeing that Julius had already made his move, and wanting to ally himself with Julius in order to weaken the Venetians, the French king judged it impossible to refuse him troops without openly offending him. Hence, by his impetuous move, Julius achieved what no other pontiff could have achieved with all the prudence in the world. Had he waited for all the negotiations to be completed and everything arranged before setting out from Rome, as any other pontiff would have done, he would never have succeeded, because by then the King of France would have discovered a thousand excuses and the others a thousand doubts. I will not touch on Pope Julius's other actions, which have all been of the same kind and have all been successful. Moreover, the shortness of his life did not allow him to experience reverses, because if times had changed so as to compel him to act with caution, he would have come to ruin, for he could never have deviated from the way nature inclined him.

Therefore, I conclude that when Fortune changes and men rigidly continue in their ways, they will flourish so long as Fortune and their ways are in accord, but they will come to ruin the moment these are in discord. In my view, however, it is better to be impetuous than cautious, because Fortune is a woman, and if you wish to dominate her you must beat and batter her. It is clear that she will let herself be won by men who are impetuous rather than by those who step cautiously. Therefore, like a woman, she is more partial to young men, because they are less cautious, wilder, and command her with greater audacity.

---

90. Giovanni Bentivoglio (1443-1508) had been Gonfalonier of Bologna until Pope Paolo II made him chief senator for life in 1466. He was expelled from Bologna in 1506 by Pope Julius II.

CHAPTER TWENTY-SIX

An exhortation to free Italy

from the barbarians

I have given much thought to all the matters I have discussed until now, and have asked myself whether the time is ripe for Italy to greet a new prince, to offer to a prudent and skilful man the prospect of forging a government that would bring him honour and benefit all Italy. So many things have come together that are favourable to a new prince that I believe there has never been a more auspicious time. As I have already said, the people of Israel had to be slaves in Egypt so that the qualities of Moses would come to the fore, and for the Medes to oppress the Persians for the greatness of Cyrus to become apparent, and for the Athenians to be dispersed so that Theseus could demonstrate his skill. In the same way, that we may see the prowess of an Italian prince, it has been necessary for Italy to be reduced to the state it is in at present: more enslaved than the Jews, more in bondage than the Persians, more dispersed than the Athenians, without a leader, without order, beaten, plundered, flayed, overrun, exposed to all manner of adversity.

We have had occasional glimmers of hope that led us to believe that a certain man might have been ordained by God to bring redemption to Italy, but then we saw him rejected by Fortune at the pinnacle of his success.[91] And so Italy has lain prostrate, waiting for a saviour who

91. Almost certainly a reference to Cesare Borgia.

would heal her wounds and put an end to the plundering of Lombardy and the taxation of Naples and Tuscany, a saviour who would cure her sores that have been festering for so long. How she prays to God to send someone to save her from the barbaric cruelty and violence! How ardent and eager she is to follow a banner, if only there were someone who would raise it high. Italy has one hope, and that hope is Your illustrious House with its Fortune and prowess, a House of which You are now the prince favoured by God and Church![92] Saving Italy would not be an insurmountable task if You kept before Your eyes the examples of Moses, Cyrus, and Theseus. Though they were extraordinary men, they were mere mortals, and they had less favourable prospects than those that Italy offers. Their campaigns were not more righteous, nor was their lot easier, nor did God look upon them with more benevolence than He looks upon You. There is great justice in our enterprise: 'The only war that is just is one that is compulsory, and weapons righteous when there is no hope but in weapons.'[93] [*Iustum enim est bellum quibus necessarium, et pia arma ubi nulla nisi in armis spes est.*] Circumstances are most favourable, and there cannot be great difficulty where circumstances are so favourable, as long as the House of Medici follows the models I have put forward. And we have seen extraordinary and unprecedented signs from God: the sea parting, a cloud showing the way, water pouring from a stone, manna raining from heaven. Everything has concurred for Your greatness. You must do the rest, for God does not want to do everything, lest he take from us our free will and that part of the glory that belongs to us.

One need not marvel that none of the Italians I have mentioned has been able to achieve what one hopes Your illustrious House will achieve. If it seems that our military prowess has been exhausted in so many upheavals and so many campaigns of war here in Italy, this is because Italy's old military institutions were not good and because there was nobody who was able to foster new ones. Nothing brings so much honour to a man who emerges as a new prince as the new laws and new institutions he creates, and when these have a sound foundation and

92. The House of Medici.
93. A slightly altered quotation from Livy, Book IX, chapter 1: *Iustum est bellum, Samnites, quibus necessarium, et pia arma, quibus nulla nisi in armis relinquitur spes.* [A war is just, Samnites, when it is compulsory, and weapons righteous when there is no hope except in weapons.]

greatness, they bring him esteem and admiration. Here in Italy there is ample matter that one can form: There is great spirit in the populace, even if it has been lacking in the leaders. Consider our duels and skirmishes, and you will see how the Italian is superior in strength, skill, and ingenuity. But when it comes to armies, the Italians have not shown themselves in the best light. All this goes back to the weakness of our commanders, because the finest among them are not followed, as every commander wants to go his own way. Until now there has been no one who has distinguished himself enough in skill or Fortune for the others to cede to him. The result has been that in the wars fought over the past twenty years, all the armies made up entirely of Italians have fared badly: the battles at Taro, Alexandria, Capua, Genoa, Vailà, Bologna, and Mestri all bear witness to this.

If Your illustrious House wishes to follow the excellent Moses, Cyrus, and Theseus who redeemed their lands, it will be vital above all else, as a true foundation of every campaign, to furnish yourself with an army of your own men. You will not find soldiers who are better, more faithful, or more true. Every man among them will be good, and all together they will become even better once they are commanded by their own prince and are honoured and treated well by him. It is necessary, therefore, to create such an army, so one can defend oneself with Italian prowess from a foreign enemy. Even though the Swiss and the Spanish infantries are considered formidable, they both have shortcomings, which is why an army that is structured differently could not only match them on the field but be confident of defeating them. This is because the Spanish cannot stand up to a cavalry, and the Swiss to an infantry that is as fierce in battle as they are. Experience has shown and will show again that the Spaniards cannot stand up to the French cavalry, and the Swiss cannot stand up to a Spanish infantry, and though there is no actual proof of the latter, some evidence of it was seen in the Battle of Ravenna, when the Spanish infantry came face to face with the German battalions, which are set up along the same lines as the Swiss. In this battle, the Spaniards with their agility and their bucklers had cut through the German pikes and were primed to destroy the Germans, who were caught completely unawares. Had the cavalry not come to their rescue, the Germans would all have been killed. Hence, if one knows the weakness in the Spanish and Swiss infantries, one should create a new infantry that can resist the cavalry and not be intimidated by other infantries. This will be made possible by the type of arms furnished to the new infantry and a change in its disposition. It is these things which, newly organized, will bring prestige and greatness to a new prince.

This opportunity must be grasped. Italy, after so many years, must welcome its liberator. The love with which these lands that have suffered a flood of foreign armies will receive him will be boundless, as will be their thirst for vengeance, their iron loyalty, their devotion and tears. All doors will be flung open. What populace would not embrace such a leader? What envy would oppose him, what Italian withhold respect? For all here abhor the barbarian dominion. Your illustrious House must seize this matter with the kind of spirit and hope in which righteous tasks are seized, so that Italy shall be ennobled beneath its banners and under its auspices the words of Petrarch will come true:

> Prowess shall take up arms
> Against brutality, and the battle will be swift;
> For ancient Roman bravery
> Is not yet dead in Italian hearts.[94]

94. *Virtù contro a furore / Prenderà l'arme, e fia el combatter corto; / Ché l'antico valore / Nell'italici cor non è ancor morto.*

NICCOLÒ MACHIAVELLI

Niccolò Machiavelli was born in Florence on 3 May 1469. Little is known about his youth but in 1498 he was nominated Secretary of the Second Chancery of the Florentine Republic. His fortunes rose over the next decade as he acted as diplomat, ambassador and negotiator for Florence's high-level relations with other Italian states and foreign powers. At what seemed to be the height of his political career, Machiavelli's fortunes changed. In 1512 the Medici returned to power in Florence and Machiavelli came under suspicion of conspiracy and was imprisoned and tortured. He was subsequently exiled from Florence.

Machiavelli spent his years of exile on his farm near San Casciano with his wife and children. Between 1512 and 1520 he produced his most famous works, *The Prince*, *The Discourses*, *The Art of War* and his plays *The Woman of Andros* and *The Mandrake*. *The Prince* is the first modern treatise of political philosophy and over the centuries it has remained an influential work. It was written as an attempt to gain favour with Lorenzo de' Medici but was unsuccessful in this aim.

In 1520 the new ruler of Florence, Giulio de' Medici, commissioned Machiavelli to carry out a diplomatic mission to Lucca. He then employed him to write what would be his last great work, *Florentine Histories*. In the last years of his life Machiavelli saw the Medici government fall and found himself out of favour once again. He died on 21 June 1527. *The Prince* was published posthumously in 1532.

ABOUT THE TRANSLATOR

Peter Constantine was awarded the 1998 PEN Translation Prize for *Six Early Stories* by Thomas Mann and the 1999 National Translation Award for *The Undiscovered Chekhov*. His widely acclaimed translation of the complete works of Isaac Babel received the Koret Jewish Literature Award and a National Jewish Book Award citation. His translation from the Greek of a poetry collection by Stylianos Harkianakis received the 2005 Hellenic Association of Translators of Literature Prize. Peter Constantine's translations of fiction and poetry have appeared in many publications, including *The New Yorker*, *Harper's* and *The Paris Review*. He lives in New York City.